We Hav
The Land

The story of the purchase by the
Assynt Crofters' Trust
of the North Lochinver Estate

To Lewis,

A very happy Christmas —

and very best wishes

John MacAskill

7th December, 1999

We Have Won
The Land

John MacAskill

The story of the purchase by the

of the North Lochinver Estate

Foreword by Dr. Jim Hunter

acair

Permission to reproduce the photographs and illustrations by courtesy of:
The Daily Telegraph (Clare Arron)
Scottish Media Newspapers Ltd.
(*The Herald* and *Evening Times* Picture Library)
Am Bratach (Donald MacLeod)
John H. Paul Photography
Hugh Webster (Scottish Highland Photo Library)
John MacPherson
Clive Sheppard
John MacAskill
Donald King
John Clegg & Co.
Assynt Crofters' Trust

Map by David Langworth

First published in 1999 by Acair Limited
7 James Street
Stornoway
Scotland
HS1 2QN

Text and cover designed by Margaret Anne Macleod.
Printed by ColourBooks Ltd., Dublin.

CONTENTS

ACKNOWLEDGEMENTS

The writing of this account of the Assynt Crofters' Trust would not have been possible without the help of many people. In particular I should like to thank John MacKenzie who was very generous with his time and gave me a considerable amount of help, not least through reading and commenting on a draft of the script and Bill Ritchie and Allan MacRae who talked to me about the project while the tape recorder whirred in front of them! Other members of the Trust, including the current Chairman Kenny MacKenzie, have also helped me, but I should like to single out Aileen Kinnaird for her immaculate handwritten minutes of meetings of the steering group and of the meetings of the crofters, and Ishbel MacAuley for having the foresight to record the television programmes concerning the purchase. Simon Fraser of Anderson, MacArthur & Co also kindly gave up his valuable time to talk to me. Professor Donald Meek and Janet Hunter from the Department of Celtic at Aberdeen University encouraged me in my venture. Dr Jim Hunter and Dr Frank Rennie both read the book in draft form and I am indebted to them for their views and comments. I should also like to thank Gillian Munro at the Scottish Office Library in Edinburgh for dealing so helpfully with my requests for documents.

None of the above, however, shares any responsibility for the views, or the errors, contained in this book.

J.H.M
Taigh nan Craobhan
Strathan
Lochinver
April, 1999

FOREWORD

Prior to the overwhelming victory won by Labour in the general election of May 1997, the party pledged itself 'to initiate a study into the system of land ownership and management in Scotland'. That pledge was honoured, in October 1997, with the establishment of the Scottish Office's Land Reform Policy Group. The Group's remit was 'to identify and assess proposals for land reform in rural Scotland'. Its Recommendations for Action were launched by the Secretary of State for Scotland Mr Donald Dewar, in January 1999.

Making clear that he hoped the Land Reform Policy Group's suggestions would constitute the basis for early legislative action by the Scottish parliament due to be elected the following May, Mr Dewar commented: 'There is, of course, still a wide range of attitudes to land reform, from those who think that any change at all is profoundly dangerous to those who think that anything short of immediate confiscation of all large landholdings is inadequate. But between those two extremes there is now a remarkable degree of agreement about what most needs to change and about what the priorities are'.

Mr Dewar continued: 'Land reform, for so long an issue out of the spotlight, has now moved firmly centre stage. On all sides, it seems to be understood that it would be most fitting for legislation on land reform to be amongst the first acts of our new Scottish parliament.'

The political momentum thus acquired by the cause of land reform is owed, in large measure, to the events described in John MacAskill's most timely book. Community ownership of the type achieved in Assynt in 1992 was not unprecedented in a Highlands and Islands context. It has existed in the Stornoway area of Lewis, for

example, since the 1920s. And with the formation of the
Scottish Crofters Union in the mid 1980s, there began to
emerge a good deal of feeling - expressed by myself among
others - to the effect that something akin to the Stornoway
model ought to be adopted more widely in the Highlands
and Islands. But it was one thing to talk, or write about, such
possibilities. It was quite another thing to take them out of
the realm of theoretical speculation and give them practical
effect. This was the great accomplishment of the Assynt
Crofters' Trust.

The extent to which Assynt's success altered the climate
of opinion with regard to community ownership in the
Highlands and Islands can be seen by comparing attitudes
prior to 1992 with developments subsequent to that date.
When, in the mid 1920s, the entire island of Lewis and
Harris was offered to its people by the island's then owner,
Lord Leverhulme, this offer - other than by residents of
Stornoway parish - was rejected. When much of Barra was
similarly offered to its occupants by MacNeil of Barra in the
1970s, rejection again followed - as it did also, though
admittedly in rather more complicated circumstances, on
government-owned crofting estates in Skye and Raasay in
the late 1980s. In the five or six years following the Assynt
breakthrough, however, community ownership of extensive
estates has been established in five separate localities: in
Borve and Annishadder in Skye; in Melness in Sutherland;
on the Isle of Eigg; in Bhaltos in Lewis and in Knoydart.
Several other packages of land - including a substantial tract
of woodland at Abriachan beside Loch Ness - have also been
taken into community ownership. And a community group
at Laggan have acquired the management of an extensive
forestry plantation in Strathmashie.

A number of the more recent community ownership
initiatives have been facilitated by the Community Land

Unit which Highlands and Islands Enterprise, the principal public sector development agency in Northern Scotland, was instructed to set up by Scottish Office minister, Brian Wilson, a man with a longstanding commitment to land reform, within months of the Labour government taking office in 1997. At the time of writing, February 1999, HIE's Community Land Unit has more that 30 'live' cases on its books - another measure of the extent to which people, right across the Highlands and Islands, are interested in following Assynt's lead.

From an HIE perspective, and I write as the agency's chairman, community land ownership is not so much an end in itself, more a means to attaining the wider economic and social development of the Highlands and Islands. At the centre of such development has to be the enhancement of collective self-confidence in rural communities which, until recently, had virtually no prospect of ever having any worthwhile say in the management of one of their most basic assets - their land. To change that situation, by bringing land under community control, is a genuinely liberating experience - as is shown by this book's sometimes moving account of how people in Assynt felt, and spoke, about their 1992 victory. That is not to say, as John MacAskill properly stresses, that community ownership is a one-way street to instant success. It is not. As Assynt folk have already discovered, making a go of community ownership is not easy. It is, in fact, extremely difficult. And I have no doubt that some experiments in community ownership will end in grief. But others will succeed - and by succeeding, they will contribute enormously to the much wider process of enabling the people of the Highlands and Islands to take more charge of their own lives, their own destinies.

Much has happened already since the day in December 1992 when Assynt crofter, Allan Macrae, was able to tell his relatives: 'We've got the land.' Much more will happen when the Scottish parliament moves, as it surely will, to give effect to the recommendations of the Scottish Office's Land Reform Policy Group.

Among the measures the group envisages are:

'Legislation to allow time to assess the public interest when major properties change hands ... The legislation would require owners to give notice of the forthcoming sale; a minimum period between notice to sell and closing date would be set; and a new power would be created for government to intervene in the public interest to impose a further period of delay to the closing date.'

'Legislation to give duly constituted community bodies a community right to buy land in areas of special importance in rural Scotland as and when it changes hands ... The legislation would provide that, when relevant property ... is offered for sale, a community group which satisfied a Scottish minister that community purchase by that group would be in the public interest could exercise a right to buy at a price to be set by a government-appointed valuer.'

'Legislation [to] give Scottish ministers a new compulsory purchase power exercisable where it appeared to them to be in the public interest. Such a provision would, for example, deter evasion of the community right to buy in circumstances such as those where shares in a company are traded, rather than the land itself.'

In relation to what has gone before, those proposals, if enacted by the Scottish parliament, will amount to a huge step forward. They will make it a lot simpler for others to follow where the Assynt Crofters' Trust so inspiringly led. And when Members of the Scottish Parliament get around, as I hope they will do very soon, to turning the Land Reform Policy Group's suggestions into law, they ought to be steered firmly in the direction of this book. Here they will find why land reform matters; why it engenders such strong feeling; why it is one of the keys to ensuring, in the Highlands and Islands especially, that the Scottish parliament takes the steps needed to make Scotland a better, freer, place.

James Hunter
February 1999

PREFACE

When the Assynt Crofters' Trust took possession of the
North Lochinver Estate on 1st February 1993 there is no
doubt that history was made. I have tried in the pages of this
book to record the events of those momentous months from
June 1992. I have also tried to place the activities of the
Assynt Crofters' Trust in their historical context and to give
some legislative background so that the purchase can be seen
in the round. I have also attempted to give a flavour of the
significance of the Assynt Crofters' Trust in the context of the
current debate on land reform and the focus on the
community. I have quoted freely from newspapers and the
media and also, in many cases, used the words of those
closely involved in the purchase, and I hope that the notes
and references which follow each chapter and the
bibliography will point those who wish to delve further,
in the appropriate direction.

CHRONOLOGY OF KEY EVENTS

1992

Early summer	Estate sale particulars are published
5th June	Decision of the Court of Session in the Whitbread case
9th June	Assynt Branch of the SCU press release as to the intention of the crofters to purchase the estate
20th June	First public meeting of Assynt crofters
28th July	Launch of the public appeal for funds
9th September	The first bid is put in by Assynt Crofters' Trust
16th September	Closing date for the first bid
22nd September	The first bid is rejected
23rd September	The second bid is put in by Assynt Crofters' Trust
30th September	The second bid is rejected
27th November	The third bid is put in by Assynt Crofters' Trust

4th December	The final bid is put in by Assynt Crofters' Trust
8th December	Announcement of the success of Assynt Crofters' Trust final bid

1993

1st February	Assynt Crofters' Trust takes possession of the estate
5th February	Celebration Cèilidh

CHAPTER 1

Introduction

• It seems we have won the land •

In the early afternoon of 8th December 1992, Simon Fraser was at his desk in his office overlooking the harbour in Stornoway when he received a telephone call from Simon Laird. Fraser recalls that Laird said that it "... looks like we have a deal." The bid by the Assynt Crofters' Trust for the North Lochinver Estate had been successful. After giving John MacKenzie the good news, he set off immediately for the afternoon flight from Stornoway to Inverness, aiming to arrive in Assynt in the evening. John MacKenzie had been sitting by the telephone at his home in Culkein Drumbeg waiting for the call; the tension of waiting had been further heightened by the presence of a television camera crew. MacKenzie recalls on hearing the news that he felt a sense of anti-climax, but that on the following day when he looked out on the land outside his croft he became conscious of what had been achieved; that his forbears would not have had the same sense of ownership of, and belonging to, the land which he now had. Allan MacRae was working on the bridge in Lochinver when he heard the news that the bid had been accepted. He was momentarily stunned but also confesses to a sense of anti-climax, and says that it took time for what they had achieved to sink in. He telephoned relations, saying simply: "We've got the land. The word has just come through."[1] Bill Ritchie had a similar reaction to John MacKenzie: "The next day, walking out over the land, it was just awesome. To think we had actually pulled it off, that this was for the first time ever, in legal terms anyway, the crofters'. That the crofters could ... get up in the morning and say 'this is ours'. That was a huge, magnificent feeling."[2]

A meeting was hastily arranged for that evening in Stoer school for the official announcement to be made. The official press release from the selling agents, embargoed until 6pm on the 8th December said simply: "After many weeks of negotiations, agreement has now been reached for the sale of the North Lochinver Estate in Sutherland to the Assynt Crofters' Trust Ltd ... It is understood that the Assynt Crofters will issue a statement at a public meeting in Assynt this evening. Both sides expressed satisfaction at the outcome. Settlement is due in February 1993."

Stoer school on the evening of 8th December was the scene of euphoric celebration of the success of the Trust's bid. The school was packed with crofters, supporters, the press and television cameras. Allan MacRae, Bill Ritchie, John MacKenzie and Simon Fraser walked up to the table at the head of the room accompanied by the accordion music of Kenny John Matheson and with the applause of the crofters ringing in their ears. Allan MacRae then said: "Well, ladies and gentlemen, it seems we have won the land. It certainly is a moment to savour; there is no doubt about that and certainly my immediate thoughts are to wish that some of our forbears could be here to share this moment with us. In winning the land, Assynt crofters have struck a historic blow for people on the land right throughout the Highlands." Bill Ritchie then spoke. Holding up a book by Iain Fraser Grigor,[3] he said that the book had been given to him by Simon Fraser at an early stage in the transaction. It described the story of the crofters' movement up to the passing of the Crofters' Holdings (Scotland) Act 1886 and it had given them all a great deal of inspiration. He then quoted from the book: "The 1886 Crofters Act represented a remarkable victory for the Highland crofters. It was not an end however but a beginning. The greatest single demand of the crofters' movement - the land to the people - was not met nor has it yet [1979] been met." Ritchie closed the book and said: "Well, they can start re-writing the history books because we have our land!"

There was nothing more to be said and the crofters then proceeded to an evening of happy and relaxed celebrations, aided by a case of whisky donated by the Culag Hotel in Lochinver, and some champagne; after all, they were now landowners and as Bill Ritchie said, perhaps they should now start learning some new habits! A song, composed by Isobel MacPhail, the daughter of one of the crofters from Clashmore, was sung to the tune of 'For These are My Mountains'. The chorus summed up the feelings:

For these are my mountains
And the crofts we all ken,
The land's for the people -
Not for sale, yet again.
So the crofters of Assynt
All met in the school -
The land's for the people
Not for landlords to rule.

The success of the crofters was reported widely and enthusiastically in the media with headlines such as 'Assynt Crofters Break Lairds' Stranglehold',[4] 'Crofters Drink to Land Victory',[5] 'Third Time Lucky in Assynt',[6] 'Crofting Trust Warms Scots Hearts Around the World',[7] 'Land for the People',[8] and 'We're the Landlords Now'![9] But the headline on the front page of *The Scotsman* of the 9th December: 'Crofters Win Battle for Estate - Tenants at Last Clinch Historic Buy-out', underneath a picture of Allan MacRae and his dog standing on a rock with a bottle of champagne held aloft, silhouetted against Suilven, in a sense said it all.[10] For here was a newspaper which, during the Crofters' War of the 19th century had been firmly on the side of the landowners, and whose sentiments one might not have expected necessarily to have been on the side of the crofters, giving an enthusiastic welcome to the victory of the Assynt crofters.[11]

By an extraordinary coincidence, Lochinver was also in the national news that day for a very different reason, albeit a reason which was a further example of the difficulties faced by the Highlands. The fishermen who sailed out of Lochinver had blockaded Lochinver Harbour on the 8th December as a protest over EC fishing regulations and the quota system and the pictures of the blockaded harbour were prominent in the press and on television. So, on the front page of the *Press & Journal* for the 9th December, Assynt had a monopoly of the headlines: 'Monro's Broadside Over Port Blockade' and 'Assynt Toasts Historic Crofts Victory', and in *The Daily Telegraph* for the same day, news of the success of the Trust was given in a story under the heading, 'Crofters Reverse Land Ownership and Buy 21,000 Acre Estate', which appeared immediately above a picture of the fishing boats lined up across the harbour entrance, itself above an article headed, 'Trawlers Blockade Port Over Fish Quotas'.

The official handover of the estate to the Trust took place on Monday 1st February 1993, when the keys to the estate (in effect the keys to Torbreck House)[12] were handed over to the Trust by Peter Voy, the factor to the Assynt Estate. There was a thanksgiving service in Stoer Free Church on the 3rd February at which the purchase of the estate was celebrated by the Reverend Fred Hurst of the Church of Scotland, the Reverend Archie MacPhail of the APC Church and the Reverend Neil MacLean of the Free Church. And in the evening of the 5th February the Trust celebrated at a grand cèilidh in the Culag Hotel in Lochinver with their friends and supporters including many representatives from the various public bodies and agencies which had been such steadfast supporters through the whole process. The success of the Assynt crofters was marked with music. In addition to Isobel MacPhail's song, two pieces of pipe music were composed; one, a pipe jig, the other a hornpipe which was to be played by the City of Glasgow Pipes and Drums in a piping competition.

But the language used by MacRae, Ritchie and MacKenzie and by the media, is striking. 'Land for the people', 'the land ... is ours', 'we have our land', 'we have won the land', talk of a historic blow being struck for people on the land throughout the Highlands. What gave rise to such depth of feeling and emotion? Why was it so important for the Assynt crofters to feel that the land was theirs? Why do the images speak of a fight for the land, of a victory? Norman MacCaig had written of the anguish concerning the land in Assynt. MacCaig, who died in 1996, had spent a considerable amount of time in Assynt; ten weeks in a cottage at Achmelvich each summer for forty five years. In his poem, 'A Man in Assynt', MacCaig shows his very clear awareness, with particular reference to Assynt, of the extent to which since the early 19th century, community and landscape in the Highlands have been broken by the forces and consequences of the clearances.[13] The poem which has been described as being somewhat political, taking the form of a discussion[14] makes a clear reference to Mr Vestey's ownership of the Assynt Estate and the sadness and injustice of lands owned in this way:

Who owns this landscape -
The millionaire who bought it or
the poacher staggering downhill in the early morning
with a deer on his back?

His repeated questions in the poem, 'Who owns this landscape?' 'Who possesses this landscape?' 'Who does the sea belong to?' his question, 'Where have they gone, the people who lived ... here?' his reference to the descendants of the Highlanders being '... kept in their place by English businessmen and the indifference of a remote and ignorant government', are all moving reminders of the agonies which the Highlands suffered in the late 18th century and in the 19th century and of the importance of the land issue in the Highlands. So also John McGrath's 1973 play 'The Cheviot, the Stag and the Black, Black Oil' which brought vividly to life the fact that the agonies of the 18th and 19th centuries were still to be found in the late 20th century Highlands and Islands, that crofters in Assynt could regard themselves as '... wholly-owned subsidiaries of the Vestey Brothers'.[15] The performance of the play in crofting communities in the early 1970s was the apotheosis of the will of the crofters, despite the centuries of agony, still to make the land their own;[16] it demonstrated that the feeling and knowledge of the people still existed and, perhaps more importantly, that their point of view had not, as it had so often in the past, been suppressed.[17]

In the immediate aftermath of the Trust's success, the words of Allan MacRae, Bill Ritchie and John MacKenzie were celebrating the fact that this will, or dream, had become reality.

What, then, is the significance of the ownership of land, the occupation of land, the use to which land in the Highlands is put and the relationship between owner and occupier? Why was it that one of the Trust's supporters had been moved to write: "Earlier this year, while consulting Dwelly's Dictionary, I chanced on 'Is treasa tuath na tighearna'[18] under the entry 'tuath'. The historic victory of the Assynt crofters demonstrates the truth of the saying."

John MacKenzie recalls being interviewed by Isabel Hilton of *The Independent* when the Trust was being set up. Why was it, she wanted to know, that it was so important to the crofters that they should own the land? Why did they have such an intense feeling for the land? MacKenzie took her to a window in his house and asked her to look outside at the lines of stones. He explained that his forbears had been cleared in 1819 from Inchnadamph, had moved to Canisp and from there to Culkein Drumbeg where his house now stood. Those stones, he said, were the remnants of the work put in by his forbears to bring into production the rough land to which they had been cleared but over which they had no rights; a stark and poignant reminder of the clearances, of the conditions which the crofters had to endure and of the work they had to put in to scratch a living from the land. Achieving ownership of the land was the realisation of a dream that the wrongs of centuries past should be rectified. Before looking in detail at the story of the purchase, we set the significance of the success of the Assynt Crofters' Trust in its historical context and look at why it is that the sense of attachment to the land is so important.

• The sense of attachment to the land •

The Battle of Culloden in April 1746 is often seen as the watershed for the breakup of the clan system and the destruction of the Highland way of life. After Culloden, "the Highlands entered a 20 year period of enclosure and cultural disintegration in which half a million people were directly, or through economic pressure, forced off the land."[19] In many ways this is so but, in truth, it is likely that the seeds of this destruction were sown earlier.[20] In the aftermath of Culloden came the well known Acts forbidding the carrying of arms (not, it may be said, for the first time), the wearing of tartan, the playing of bagpipes and the abolition of the private courts held by the landowners (the heritable jurisdictions), and the forfeiture of estates (again, not for the first time), held by the rebel landowners.

But the legislative and cultural attack on the Gaidhealtachd had begun even earlier - in the seventeenth century with the Statutes of Iona of 1609, which outlawed the carrying of arms, forced the chiefs to establish presbyterian churches and effectively outlawed the Gaelic bards, followed in 1616 by the Act for the settling of Parochial Schools whose declared aim was to do away with the Gaelic language.[21]

There can be little doubt that the actions taken and the attitudes adopted after Culloden were crucial in the break-up of the Highland way of life. While the attack on the cultural aspects of this way of life - dress, music, language - were of course important it was the realisation that land was a commercial asset which was fundamental. It was this shift in the attitude of the landowners in the Highlands and Islands to their land and its commercial value, and market pressures, which was at the root of the destruction of the Highland way of life and the eventual creation of the crofting community.

Market pressures, the industrialisation of the Lowlands and a need on the part of the Highland chiefs to maximise their income led to 'commercial landlordism'[22] or the 'commoditization'[23] of land in the Highlands: "... with the abolition of the heritable jurisdictions in 1747, having brought the Highland chieftains within the pale of the law, and placed them on the same footing as the other gentlemen of the land, they began rapidly to acquire the same tastes, to be occupied with the same pursuits, to feel the same desires, and to have the same wants as their brethren in the south. In order however to indulge in their propensities, and to be able to appear in the capital with due effect, it was necessary that they should convert their estates to the mode of occupation most suited to their circumstances, and from which they could derive the greatest income."[24] But this process had been underway long before Culloden. The Duke of Argyll had instituted competitive bidding for leases in the decade before Culloden providing a "... model for the commercial re-orientation of estate management at the expense of clanship ..."[25] and the assimilation of Highland chiefs into Scottish landed society which resulted in growing absenteeism and the accumulation of debts which could not be satisfied by the low rental levels had begun even earlier, in the 17th century: " ... the Restoration era was to witness a fundamental shift in the nature and structure of clanship away from traditionalism towards commercialism."[26] "Absentee landlordism, indebtedness, rent-raising and the removal and relocation of clansmen were not products of the 'Forty-Five', but part of an ongoing process of commercialism and cultural assimilation that can be traced back to the early seventeenth century."[27]

And so the sheep came and the people were moved to marginal plots of land around the coast and the crofting community was created. When the sheep on the cleared lands became unprofitable, deer forests were created, but again not to the benefit of the crofter. The lost lands were not returned. The Napier Commission asked Evander McIver, the then Sutherland estate factor, a question about the conversion of sheep farms into deer forests when the sheep farm could no longer be let. "It is a very difficult thing to get a sheep farm off [the Duke's hands], and he converted it [Glencanisp] into a deer forest."[28] No question of the lands going back to the people. Murdoch Kerr of Achmelvich, when asked before the Napier Commission which of the two he preferred, sheep or deer, replied: "Have they not both been the destruction of the place to us? Have they not sent us down to the rocks and the shore of the sea?"[29]

Commoditization of land in Assynt in the 1800s led to eviction and dispossession on a large scale and this of itself caused great anguish. But it was not just the fact of dispossession, the physical loss of home and land, that caused this anguish. The commoditization of land also violated the principle of *dùthchas.*

Traditionally, under the tribal basis of Highland clanship, the chief was considered to be under a moral obligation towards his clansmen to provide protection and security of possession for them on his lands, in return for which the clansmen would fight for him.[30] There was a belief that the prolonged occupation of the land gave rise to a right of permanent tenancy of it - *dùthchas.*[31] The chief, then, would not regard the land as a commercial asset. The word *tuath* in the Gaelic motto of the Highland Land Law Reform Association also looks back to the world of the *tuath,* the basic unit of civilisation, and to those very much earlier days when the " ... occupants of land were thought to have claims on that land which transcended those even of their king."[32] The clearances were a direct violation of this principle.[33] What is the evidence for the principle?[34]

At the hearing of the Napier Commission at Lochinver on 27th July 1883, there was an interchange between the Commission and the Reverend Norman Mackay who was giving evidence on behalf of the Assynt crofters and cottars which went as follows:-

Commission: "What is the exact meaning you attach to the word 'proprietor' ... ?"

Mackay: "An owner of land."

Commission: "... What do you mean by ownership?"

Mackay: "That the possessor has a right to the property, to the goods or to the property."

Commission: "And has an occupier an equal right?"

Mackay: "In the Highlands I consider that the peasantry have a far greater right than elsewhere. In the case of a chief or head of a clan, I think the head of that clan came very likely into the position in which he finds himself through the assistance of the crofters all around about him. He and they have grown up upon the land; they have made him chief, and he has always felt that it was his duty to protect them. I don't say that either the chiefs or tenants have now the same feeling; still, I may say this before the Commission that I find the regard for clanship strong in the people here, and they are very loath to give up the idea that their proprietor won't do everything possible for them ... "[35]

In its Report the Napier Commission itself said: "The opinion so often expressed before us that the small tenantry of the Highlands have an inherited inalienable title to security of tenure in their possessions, while rent and service are duly rendered, is an impression indigenous to the country, though it has never been sanctioned by legal recognition, and has never been long repudiated by the action of the proprietor."[36]

The Commission made reference to the writings of two earlier commentators, Captain Edward Burt and the Earl of Selkirk. Captain Burt, in his *Letters from a Gentleman in the North of Scotland* published in 1759 referred to the notion that the clansmen had "... a kind of hereditary right to their farms; and that none of them are to be dispossessed, unless for some great transgression against their chief, in which case every individual would be content to their expulsion."[37] The Earl of Selkirk, in his *Observations on the Present State of the Highlands of Scotland* written in 1805, said: "The permanent possession which [the Highland tenants] had always retained of their paternal farms, they consider as their just right, from the share they had borne in the general defence, and can see no difference between the title of the chief and their own."[38]

Notwithstanding this the Napier Commission went on to say that: "We are bound to express the opinion that a claim to security of tenure, founded in the old usage of the country, cannot now be seriously entertained."[39] In the event, of course, the Crofters' Holdings (Scotland) Act 1886 did grant security of tenure and this fundamental legal right has remained ever since and, indeed, has been built on. But while the Commission may not have considered the claim could seriously be entertained, the leaders of the crofters at the time of the Crofters' War did not doubt the existence of this inalienable right and the fact that security of tenure was eventually granted pays tribute to their firmness of purpose. John Murdoch, the radical and charismatic editor of *The Highlander* was clear on the issue and the evidence for it: "It is in the Gaelic language that we have, as in some of the songs of Iain Lom ... in tradition, and in proverbs - a distinct recognition of the fact that the lands in the Highlands belonged to the clans as such, and not to the chiefs."[40]

While the Gaelic poets of the period of the land agitation in the 1870s and 1880s do not, in general, elaborate the argument that the land was the property of the people and not of any feudal superior, there are, nonetheless, clear references to the argument in the verse of John Smith, Mary MacPherson and John Maclean.[41] For example, in 'Teachdairean na Banrighinn' (The Queen's Commissioners), a song composed by John Maclean after the Napier Commission visited Tiree on 7th August 1883, we see a strong reference to the argument that the land belongs to the Highlanders: "Since the sheep have created a wilderness, along with the raising of rents and tributes, glens, straths and moors are uninhabited save for a shepherd and his dog. It [i.e. the Highlands] is the cradle of the children of the Gael, a healthy high land of fresh streams, and they have a right to it so old that history cannot relate it."[42]

And in John Maclean's song 'Oran nam Prìosanach' (Song of the Prisoners) composed around October 1886 after eight Tiree crofters had been sentenced for their part in the land agitations, we see the words: "Before the Duke arrived there [a reference to the Campbells who bought Tiree] or any of his ancestors or royal George of the family of Hanover, the low lying island with its many shielings belonged to the Highlanders as a dwelling place."[43]

But it was not just the Gaelic language, its traditions, proverbs and poetry which provided this evidence. Murdoch also used the Bible. He compiled a pamphlet in 1883 entitled, in English, 'The Land Question Answered from the Bible'. He drew together in this pamphlet a number of selected passages from the Bible to provide the crofters with Biblical evidence of their claim against the landlords.[44] And Norman Stewart, a crofter from Valtos in Skye who was the secretary of his local branch of the Highland Land Law Reform Association, said to a mass meeting of the branch: "If the landlords consulted Moses or Joshua, they would find there substantial evidence as to who are the rightful owners of the soil. The Lord Advocate and Sheriff Ivory [a reference to the two people most hated by the crofters for their actions in bringing proceedings against crofters in the Crofters' War] can quote Acts George and James, but we can quote the Act of God - the Bible."[45] The crofters sincerely believed that the Bible did show that their claim to the land was valid.[46]

Nor was it just the crofters, their leaders and the Gaelic poets who did not doubt this right to land. While as a matter of law, the belief in this right might have no foundation, it certainly did, in the opinion of Gladstone, have foundation as a historical fact. In his formulation of the Irish land legislation, Gladstone had used the principle of a historical customary right to land. He would extend this principle to the Highlands and Islands, arguing that the crofters had a historic title to land: "For it is, after all, this historical fact that constitutes the crofters' title to demand the interference of Parliament. It is not because they are poor or because there are too many of them, or because they want more land to support their families, but because those whom they represent had rights of which they have been surreptitiously deprived to the injury of the community."[47] The Earl of Selkirk referred to the fact that right to land arose from the share the Highlanders had had in the general defence of the clan. When, in the late eighteenth and in the nineteenth century, scores of Highlanders were recruited to the Highland regiments, it is interesting that military service and a right to land were again linked - at least in the eyes of the Highlander. Assynt was a recruiting area for the 93rd Sutherland Highlanders, the last regiment to be raised in the old way as a clan levy and thus, perhaps, the last real Highland regiment.[48] Apparently, in 1799 recruitment for the regiment was slow and this irritated the Countess of Sutherland. Indeed it has been suggested that the reluctance of the Highlanders in the area to come forward may have been instrumental in the formulation of the attitude of the Countess towards the development of the Sutherland estate and so the clearances in the area.[49] The Countess told her agent that if the people did not come forward for service, "... they need no longer be considered as a credit to Sutherland, or any advantage over sheep or any useful animal."[50] In any event, those recruited from Assynt certainly believed that part of the bargain was that if they joined up, their parents would remain securely on the land, as evidence to the Napier Commission showed: "In Assynt the great majority joined the army on the distinct under-standing that their parents would be kept in their holdings; but on the return of the survivors, they found their parents huddled together on the seashore, eking out a miserable existence, and their former holdings converted into so many sheep walks. For example, Roderick MacKenzie of Ardvar was assured that, if his two sons, William and Colin, would enlist, he would be kept in possession of his holding, but when they came home they found their parents endeavouring to exist on a miserable patch in Clachtoll,"[51] and "The general grievance in this parish [Assynt] is insufficiency and badness of land. This state of things was brought about by the Sutherland clearances which Sutherland men would like to forget. But one point to which I should like to draw attention is that in Assynt about the beginning of this century the great majority of young men joined the former 93rd on the distinct understanding that their parents would not be removed out of their holdings during their life; but when the survivors returned, they found that the promise had been broken, and that the parents for whose sake they had enlisted, had been deprived of their land, and were eking out a miserable life on barren spots along the sea shore."[52]

The contradiction of the Sutherland estate extracting military service from the people while at the same time redesigning the entire system upon which the obligations of military service were based was stark indeed.[53]

Robert MacLeod, a crofter from Carloway in Lewis, showed the depth of the sense of attachment to land felt by the crofter. In evidence to the Taylor Commission[54] in the early 1950s, he said: "As a crofter, I have great difficulty in conceding to the proprietor any greater right to the croft than I have myself. It is the four small acres my family broke in from the wild morass and rock, drained, manured and fed over the years with no help from the proprietor ... I hold this individual piece of land to be mine morally and to be disposed of as I wish."[55]

And so when Allan MacRae said at the time of the purchase by the Trust, "I think that for those of us native to

Assynt particularly, we are very conscious that the land we stand on is in a sense the last stronghold of the native people ... these lands really are the remnants of what the natives once possessed,"[56] he was echoing the thoughts and emotions of previous generations of Highlanders, and when, on 8th December 1992 he spoke of his wish that his forbears could have been there to share the moment, when John MacKenzie's immediate thoughts on hearing the news of the success of the Trust were for his forbears, when Bill Ritchie quoted from Iain Fraser Grigor's book, they were emphasising the importance of the historical context of the success of the Assynt Crofters' Trust.

Notes

1   *The Crofter,* February, 1993
2   Quoted in *BBC Landward,* November, 1993
3   Grigor, Iain Fraser, *Mightier Than A Lord,* Stornoway, 1979
4   *WHFP,* 11th December, 1992
5   *The Herald,* 9th December, 1992
6   *Press & Journal* 9th December, 1992
7   *The Independent,* 12th December, 1992
8   *Am Bratach,* January, 1993
9   *Daily Record,* 9th December, 1992
10 This picture was, in fact, taken before the news that the Trust had been successful came through and, just in case the news was bad, another picture had been taken of Allan MacRae with his head in his hands!
11 John MacKenzie, however, believes that the attitude of *The Scotsman* has not, in fact, changed from that of the 19th century newspaper
12 Torbreck House is also sometimes referred to as Torbreck Lodge
13 Hunter, James, *On The Other Side Of Sorrow,* Edinburgh, 1995, p. 134
14 McNeill, Marjory, *Norman MacCaig - A Study of His Life and Work,* Edinburgh, 1996, p. 82
15 McGrath, John, *The Cheviot, the Stag and the Black, Black Oil,* Skye, 1975, p. 27
16 Hunter, James, *The Claim of Crofting,* Edinburgh, 1991, p. 224
17 McGrath, John, There are many Truths, in Maclean, Malcolm and Connell, Christopher (Eds), *As An Fhearann,* Stornoway, 1986, p40
18 The Gaelic motto of the Highland Land Law Reform Association (later the Highland Land League), an English translation of which is 'tenantry are stronger than a laird'. The Association was formed in February 1883 to seek for crofters fair rents, security of tenure, compensation for improvements and redistribution of land. It arose out of the Crofters' War of the 1880s and in 1883 came the appointment of the Napier Commission into the condition of the crofters and cottars in the Highlands and Islands under the chairmanship of Lord Napier. The Napier Commission report gave rise eventually to the passage of the Crofters Holdings (Scotland) Act 1886 which is still the cornerstone of crofting legislation in the Highlands and Islands today.
19 McIntosh, Alastair, Wightman, Andy and Morgan, Daniel, Reclaiming the Scottish Highlands - Clearance, Conflict and Crofting, *The Ecologist,* vol 24, No 2, 1994, p. 64
20 Devine, T.M., *Clanship to Crofters' War - The Social Transformation of the Scottish Highlands,* Manchester and New York, 1994, p. 32, Macinnes, Allan I., Scottish Gaeldom: The First Phase of Clearance, in T. M. Devine and R. Mitchison, (Eds), *People and Society in Scotland,* 1, 1750-1850, Edinburgh, 1988, p. 71; and see Macinnes, Allan I., *Clanship, Commerce and the House of Stuart,* 1603-1788, East Lothian, 1996
21 Durkacz, V. E., *The Decline of the Celtic Languages,* Edinburgh, 1996, p. 4. See also Macinnes, Allan I., *Clanship, Commerce and the House of Stuart,* East Lothian, 1996, p. 65. It has been suggested recently that the Statutes of Iona should not be regarded as a turning point but rather as just one part of the gradual and continuous pressure on Highland chiefs in many related ways between 1596 and 1617; see Goodare, Julian, The Statutes of Iona in context, *The Scottish Historical Review,* volume LXXVII, I: No 203, April, 1998, p. 57

22 Macinnes, Allan I., *Clanship Commerce and the House of Stuart,* East Lothian, 1996, pp. 221-228 and Dodgshon, Robert A., *From Chiefs to Landlords,* Edinburgh, 1998, pp. 239-243

23 McIntosh, Alastair, Wightman, Andy and Morgan, Daniel, Reclaiming the Scottish Highlands - Clearance, Conflict and Crofting, in *The Ecologist,* vol 24, No 2, 1994, p. 16

24 Loch, James, *An Account of the Improvements on the Estates of the Marquess of Stafford,* London, 1820, pp. xvi and xvii

25 Macinnes, Allan I., *Clanship, Commerce and the House of Stuart,* East Lothian, 1996, p. 214 and see also Cregeen, Eric, The Tacksman and their Successors, *Scottish Studies,* 13, 1969

26 Macinnes, Allan I., The impact of the civil wars and interregnum: Political disruption and social change within Scottish Gaeldom, in R. Mitchison and P. Roebuck, (Eds), *Economy and Society in Scotland and Ireland, 1500-1939,* Edinburgh, 1988, p. 58

27 Macinnes, Allan I., *Clanship, Commerce and the House of Stuart, 1603-1788,* East Lothian, 1996 p. x

28 *Napier Report,* Q27671

29 *Napier Report,* Q27639

30 Devine, T.M., *Clanship to Crofters' War - The Social Transformation of the Scottish Highlands,* Manchester and New York, 1994, p. 11

31 The word *dùthchas* is not, in fact, an easy one to define. It is a word, however, which is full of significance to the Gaelic community. At the tenurial level it may be taken to mean "... the collective heritage of a holding in which it was believed that any holding or plot, having been held and continuously worked by a family group over four generations, belonged by customary right to those tenants." (Withers, Charles. W.J., *Urban Highlanders - Highland-Lowland Migration and Urban Gaelic Culture, 1700-1900,* East Lothian, 1998, p. 54 footnote 32; see also the article quoted in the footnote, Withers, Charles, 'Give us land and plenty of it': the ideological basis to land and landscape in the Scottish Highlands, in *Landscape History,* 12, 1990, particularly p. 49 and Withers, Charles W. J., *Gaelic Scotland - The Transformation of a Crofting Region,* London, 1988, pp. 331, 389 and 414 and Dodgshon, R., *Land and Society in Early Scotland,* Oxford, 1981, pp. 109-113). But the word conveys much more than this. The Highland, Gaelic speaking community has an internal view of itself which is largely responsible for the maintenance of its Gaelic identity; it has a strong sense of self understanding and identity and at the heart of this self understanding and identity is the concept of *dùthchas.* It is a word packed with significance - what is passed down in ones blood, ones patrimony, what comes to a person by virtue of being who that person is within a particular kindred. It includes the traditions and ways of acting and of seeing the world. It conveys a sense of belonging. The link between the word *dùthaich,* meaning a particular country or locality, and the word *dùthchas* is of quite basic significance and helps to explain why native Highlanders have often had such a deep attachment to their own locality. The land sustains the *dùthchas,* but the *dùthchas* helps to sustain the land. At its more fundamental level, *dùthchas* defined the family traits and a member of the family was measured according to these standards. The affirmation of *dùthchas* is seen in the words of the Gaelic poets, in songs and in the language, and proverbs and proverbial sayings were one of the ways by which the concept of *dùthchas* was defined and elaborated in the Gaelic context. (I would like to acknowledge my debt to

Professor Meek for my attempt here to describe the significance of
dùthchas. I have benefited greatly from his views on the subject. It is, of
course, a subject which can in no way be done justice in a footnote.)

32 Hunter, James, *On the Other Side of Sorrow*, Edinburgh, 1995, p. 65

33 Devine, T. M., *Clanship to Crofters' War - The social transformation of the
Scottish Highlands*, Manchester and New York, 1994, p. 34

34 See, generally, Hunter, James, *The Making of the Crofting Community*,
Edinburgh, 1976 pp. 156 to 160

35 *Napier Report*, Q27009 to 27011

36 *Napier Report*, p. 8

37 Burt, E. J., *Letters from a Gentleman in the North of Scotland*, London, 1759,
vol II, p. 173

38 Douglas, T., (Earl of Selkirk), *Observations on the Present State of the Highlands
of Scotland*, London, 1805, p. 120

39 *Napier Report*, p. 8

40 *The Highlander*, 8th December 1877, p. 4, quoted in Durkacz,V. E.,
The Decline of the Celtic Languages, Edinburgh, 1983, p. 207

41 Meek, Donald E., Gaelic Poets of the Land Agitation, *Transactions of the
Gaelic Society of Inverness*, vol 49, 1976, p. 323

42 Quoted in Meek, Donald E., Gaelic Poets of the Land Agitation,
Transactions of the Gaelic Society of Inverness, vol 49, 1976, p. 375

43 Meek, Donald E., *Tuath Is Tighearna, Tenants and Landlords*, Edinburgh,
1995, pp. 158 and 260 and Meek, Donald E., Gaelic Poets of the Land
Agitation, *Transactions of the Gaelic Society of Inverness*, vol 49, 1976, p. 376

44 Meek, Donald E., The Land Question Answered from the Bible; The Land
Issue and the Development of a Highland Theology of Liberation,
Scottish Geographical Magazine, vol 103, No 2, 1987, p. 87

45 *The Oban Times*, 21st February, 1885, quoted in Hunter, James,
The Making of the Crofting Community, Edinburgh, 1976, p. 159 and Meek,
Donald E., The Land Question Answered from the Bible; The Land Issue
and the Development of a Highland Theology of Liberation, *Scottish
Geographical Magazine*, vol 103, No 2, 1987, p. 88

46 Hunter, James, *The Making of the Crofting Community*, Edinburgh, 1976,
p. 159

47 Cameron, E. A., *Land for the People? The British Government and the Scottish
Highlands, c 1880-1925*, East Lothian, 1996, p. 33

48 Prebble, John, *Mutiny - Highland regiments in Revolt 1743-1804*, London,
1977, p. 501

49 Richards, Eric, The Sutherland Clearances, in *Northern Studies*, vol 2,
Number 1, 1974-75, p. 61

50 Adam, R. J., *Papers on Sutherland Estate Management*, Edinburgh, 1972,
vol 1, p xxix

51 *Napier Report*, Q27232

52 *Napier Report*, Q27266

53 Richards, Eric, The Sutherland Clearances, *Northern Studies*, vol 2,
Number 1, 1974-75, p. 65

54 *Commission of Enquiry into Crofting Conditions*, 1952-54

55 Quoted in Hunter, James, *The Claim of Crofting*, Edinburgh, 1991, p. 34

56 Quoted in McIntosh, Alastair, Wightman, Andy and Morgan, Daniel, The
Scottish Highlands in Colonial and Psychodynamic Perspective,
Interculture, Summer 1994, Issue 124, p. 33

CHAPTER 2

The Story of the Purchase
We have history, morality and the law on our side
and we are determined

• Introduction •

The North Lochinver Estate lies, as can be seen from the map on page 100, in the North West Highlands of Scotland and comprises land running from the Point of Stoer along the coast eastwards towards Kylesku as far as Loch Nedd and then south west towards Lochinver and back up the coast to Stoer Head. Oldany Island does not form part of the estate and nor, either, does the land immediately north of Loch Inver, i.e. Baddidaroch, Ardroe, Achmelvich or, indeed, the land immediately inland of Clachtoll beach. These areas (apart from Oldany Island) still form part of the Assynt Estate owned by Edmund Vestey.

It is an area of some 21,132 acres and in the words of the 1992 sale particulars is, 'An important estate of astonishing beauty and variety in a wonderful position on the North West Seaboard.' It is 'unspoilt highland/coastal scenery' with 'infinite scenic variety' a 'wilderness' with 'abundant wildlife' and a 'world famous coastline including [the] Old Man of Stoer, good sheltered moorings and outstanding boating opportunities, islands, coves, cliffs and sandy beaches'.

It is, of course, also, and primarily, a crofting area although the reader of the sale particulars could have been forgiven if this had escaped his attention. The reference to crofting in the particulars appeared in relation to estate income (the total for the estate being £2,608 per annum). There was no indication of the physical extent of the croft lands and common grazings. Within the North Lochinver Estate there are thirteen crofting townships: Torbreck, Achmelvich,[1] Clachtoll, Clashmore, Balchladich, Raffin, Achnacarnin, Culkein, Stoer, Clashnessie, Drumbeg, Culkein Drumbeg and Nedd. There are some 172 crofts and just over 140 crofters within the estate (a number of crofters within the estate owning more than one croft) and the total croft lands and common grazings within the estate account for all but 50 of the 21,132 acres.[2] Some 400 people live on the Estate, about a quarter of whom are permanent non-crofting residents. There are some 300 houses on the Estate of which some 76 are holiday homes.

The coastal area between Inverkirkaig to the south of Lochinver on the Sutherland/Ross and Cromarty border round to Nedd was one of the resettlement areas for the clearances in Assynt in the early nineteenth century and it seems that the traditional runrig system of farming was used here until the late 1840s when the townships were reorganised into crofts following the potato famine. The settlement patterns in Stoer and Clashnessie retain evidence of the old runrig system.[3] This is not the story of the clearances or of the creation of the crofting community, stories which are well told in many other places.[4] However we have seen the overall importance of the land issue and we should also look at recollections of some of the clearances in Assynt and the feelings generated by those clearances, in particular in those areas within the North Lochinver Estate, because those feelings are highly relevant to our story of the Assynt Crofters' Trust.

In his report of 13th August 1811 to the Sutherland Estate, William Young, the then estate factor, said this of Assynt: "I have no hesitation to say that to turn the greater part of this Parish to the best account it should be under Cheviot Sheep, reserving accommodation for Kelp makers, Fishermen,

Lime burners, and other Labourers ... aware as I am that Lord and Lady Stafford will in this and other districts rather sacrifice their interest than that the people should be entirely dispossessed I have in arranging the grounds for a new set keeped them in view."[5]

But dispossession on a large scale there was with most clearances taking place in two phases - in 1812 and 1819, during which times over 150 households were cleared to the coastal strip between Inverkirkaig and Nedd, the lands which now form the North Lochinver Estate in the main forming the resettlement areas for the clearances, rather than clearances taking place from these lands (apart from the case of one or two townships). The Reverend Norman Mackay, in his evidence to the Napier Commission, said that some three quarters of the area of the Parish of Assynt which was previously occupied became unoccupied following the clearances.[6] In his evidence to the Napier Commission, Kenneth Campbell, a cottar from Balchladich spoke of 48 townships in Assynt being cleared for sheep farmers with Ardvar being the last township in the parish to be cleared some 50 years before.[7] One of the families cleared to Torbreck included William MacRae, the great grandfather of Allan MacRae. Campbell spoke warmly of the places from which the clearances had taken place; they were "... the very best of places ... they were all good for the number of people that were there." The places to which the people were sent "... were not by any means good, in most cases ... some were sent to America, some to Ross-shire, some to the rocks upon the sea shore."[8]

William MacKenzie of Clashnessie told the Napier Commission that: "This state of things was brought about by a process which Sutherland men would like to forget, if the process had been reversed, and the evil remedied, by the use of means which have made the ears of savages, let alone

Christians tingle. Over fifty townships in this parish were made desolate, and the tenants sent hither and thither over the face of the earth, and when they found a resting place at all in their native land, it was on the poorest scraps, rocks, and bogs, and often put in amongst the poorest crofters, subdividing their lots, and intensifying their poverty."[9]

We turn now to Clashmore. The Duke of Sutherland wanted to turn the township of Clashmore into a farm which would demonstrate to the tenants the principles of good farming and cropping. There were some eighteen families removed in the 1870s from the farm for this purpose. If we take the evidence of Evander McIver to the Napier Commission at its face value, it was a remarkably ad hoc decision and way of dealing with the livelihood of these people. "Clashmore was a township with a lot of small tenants in it. They cultivated the lots very partially, and the Duke of Sutherland one day, standing on the hill pasture, asked me, would it not be a good thing for the employment of the people if we were to set agoing a small farm here, on which we could show the people what crops could be grown by proper trenching and drainage, and farming on the regular rotation."[10] In the event the farm largely failed; it was in a bad spot and difficult to improve. But the land was not returned to the people - the farm was let to Mr Brown the tenant of the hotel in Lochinver. The Napier Commission told Mr McIver, "I am afraid it was rather an unfortunate day when you and the Duke were looking down from the hill?" McIver answered, "It was unfortunate for the Duke, but it was fortunate for the people who were employed to make it." The Napier Commission retorted, "Was it fortunate for those poor people whose land it was?" McIver replied, "Perhaps it was not."[11]

Given this background, it is no surprise that the Clashmore farm should, during the land reform movement

of the 1880s, become a focus for the crofters' anti-landlord
activities and their demand for the return of lands. This is a
story told elsewhere;[12] but involving as it did the serving of
summonses for rent arrears, the christening by the press of
one of the ring leaders, Hugh Kerr, as the 'Sutherland Rob
Roy',[13] a gunboat being sent to Lochinver from where a
combined force of police and marines marched to
Clashmore, it serves as another illustration of the depth of
feelings in Assynt about the activities of the landlord.

• The 1989 sale •

From 1936 the Assynt estate, including the land forming the
North Lochinver Estate was, bit by bit, purchased by the
Vestey family from Mr. W. Filmer-Sankey who had himself
been given the estate by the Duke of Westminster as a
wedding present,[14] but in 1989 Edmund Vestey re-named the
coastal crofting strip comprising the thirteen crofting
townships as the 'North Lochinver Estate' and put it up for
sale as part of a strategy, in the words of Edmund Vestey, to
"... get [the Assynt estate] into the most sensible management
shape."[15] The Assynt estate wanted to acquire more hill land
and, in order to finance the purchase, the estate sold 'that bit
of the coastal country'. Might there not, perhaps, be sensed
the echo of history in this sale? In the mid 19th century, this
'bit of the coastal country' was not deemed economically
productive enough for the Sutherland Estate and was used as
the receiving area for crofters cleared from the productive
hills and glens of the interior. Now at the end of the 20th
century, this land was sold, as it were, over the heads of the
crofters to finance the purchase of the more productive hill
ground. The estate was put up for sale in three lots - the
Torbreck estate, the Drumbeg estate and the Stoer estate.
The guide price for the sale was £750,000. The price at

which the estate was eventually sold was £1,080,000. The sale in 1989 can be seen as the beginning of a concern among the crofters at the possible fragmentation of estate land and the administrative and practical problems (not to mention the underlying issues of Highland land ownership) which this would bring. The sale of part of the Assynt Estate was a fragmentation on its own, but the possibility that the estate might be sold in three lots with three new landlords taking over was a particular worry to the crofters. Bill Ritchie recalls that there was a concern that this might be the beginning of something new in the area. However, at this stage the crofters took no action of their own and, in the event, the estate was sold as a whole to Scandinavian Property Services Limited, a Company set up by a Swede, Mr Setterburg.[16] However, although no specific action was taken by the crofters on this sale, it appears that John MacKenzie was the only crofter formally to protest about the fact that, after the disposal, the crofters were unable to deal with a local factor. The management of the estate passed to Savilles based in Brechin. MacKenzie wrote a letter of protest to the new factor and to the former factor. His letter to the former factor of the estate was returned with the words: "John, you are the only person on the estate to have complained."[17] A debate was, however, taking place within the Assynt Branch of the Scottish Crofters Union about the threat of possible fragmentation of croft lands and the implications. Bill Ritchie, John MacKenzie and Allan MacRae were, respectively, the Treasurer, Vice Chairman and Chairman of the Branch and so when in 1992 rumours began to spread that SPS had gone into liquidation and the North Lochinver Estate was to be sold, it was within the Assynt Branch of the SCU that the early discussions of the implications of these rumours took place.

• The estate is again put up for sale •

John MacKenzie recalls that it was around June of 1992 that the crofters became aware of the presence of aircraft and helicopters over the area in excess of the usual low overflying by military aircraft. Donald King of Clashnessie remembers a seaplane landing in Clashnessie Bay in July and taxiing onto the beach. It carried a titled family and an Iranian gentleman who, apparently, was interested in acquiring the estate. They were told by the crofters that a purchaser would be buying nothing but croft lands (although one wonders how much this would have meant to the Iranian) and there was nothing in which a purchaser would be interested. They were suitably discouraged and flew away, although not before enjoying a champagne picnic on the beach and having the plane rescued from the soft sand by a local crofter's tractor. An early success for the crofters!

The particulars were published in the early summer of 1992 and showed that the estate was being put up for sale on the order of the liquidator of SPS and furthermore, that it was for sale not as in 1989, in three lots, but this time in seven lots. They were: the Torbreck estate, the Stoer peninsula, 208 Clashmore (a decrofted cottage), Phollain Bheithe lying to the south east of Oldany Island, Culkein Drumbeg, Drumbeg and Nedd. The guide price was £473,000. This threatened fragmentation of the estate was a serious concern to the crofters. On the administrative level it might mean that the crofters would have not just one landlord to deal with but perhaps two or more because in some instances the boundaries of the lots appeared to cut across common grazings. Furthermore, it might also mean that the crofters would be dealing not with a professional factor but with one or more owners who had no knowledge or understanding of crofting legislation. This was not

something which would be welcomed by the crofters given
that the position of the landlord is one which involves not
just important rights but also responsibilities and duties
under the legislation.[18]

While at the emotional level the landlord/tenant
relationship may still suffer from the historical burdens we
saw in Chapter 1, crofters have, in general, been content as
a practical matter to leave the landlord/tenant relationship
unchanged, in particular where they have not felt threatened
by the policies and actions of the landlord and especially
where there may be said to be a paternalistic, non intrusive
pattern of landlordism - for example as represented by the
Secretary of State for Scotland on the DAFS estates. We shall
see in Chapter 5 how little enthusiasm there has been on
these estates for the concept of community ownership. Very
few crofters have used the right to buy provisions of the
crofting legislation. In Assynt, while relations between the
crofters and the landlord and his factor may not have been
ideal, there was nothing in particular which threatened the
crofter or got in the way of the day to day running of his
croft. There was one landlord and one professional factor.
As we have seen, the 1989 sale disturbed the status quo and,
although the threatened fragmentation had not then
occurred (apart, of course from the fact that the Assynt Estate
was split up), the crofters had not found the change of
landlord helpful. John MacKenzie recalls that it was almost
a year after the sale before the arrangements made for
running the estate were made clear to the crofters and, as we
have seen, the estate was no longer managed locally, but in
Brechin. In light of this the prospect of further disturbance
and of the estate being broken up into seven parts and across
common grazings boundaries was clearly disturbing.

Whereas in 1989 there had been an undercurrent of
concern, in 1992 this concern was clearly at the surface.

Interviewed on the BBC Landward programme 'Lights in the Glen'[19] Bill Ritchie described this proposed fragmentation as a changed pattern. "We are no longer looking at the traditional relationship between the landlord who has a very large estate of which crofting is a part. What we have got here is the breaking up and selling of the croft lands in small lots. We just don't think that's the way crofting should be going. It is a breach of trust, we believe, in the traditional relationship between the crofting tenants and the landlords. We want to retain the crofting lands as a complete unit. We think there is an enormous opportunity here to demonstrate that crofters can run their own lands collectively." In making this statement, Bill Ritchie was demonstrating a refreshing degree of self confidence and willingness to take the initiative, on the part of crofters. The idea of taking responsibility for the management of a crofting estate was a new development for the crofting community. As James Hunter said in an article in *The Scotsman*,[20] while crofters had had a long standing suspicion of landlords, they had, in the past, rejected the idea of managerial control - as in Lewis and Harris in the 1920s, Barra in the 1970s and in Skye and Raasay in the early 1990s.[21]

• A wilderness where man is the alien •

The 1989 sale had been a shock to the crofters and so, in a sense, the publication of the 1992 sale particulars was seed corn being sown on fertile ground. The Assynt Branch of the SCU was active and there were three intelligent and charismatic members in Bill Ritchie, John MacKenzie and Allan MacRae who brought together an important combination of different skills and passions. Would things have been different if the estate had been offered in one lot? Would they have been different if any one or more of

Ritchie, MacKenzie and MacRae had not been there? It really is not possible to be sure. But it is clear that, in Assynt in 1992, there existed the conditions for action by the crofters. The fact of possible fragmentation was bad enough but the way in which the particulars of sale were written certainly added to the determination of the crofters on this occasion to take action. In fairness, the details of the 1992 particulars are virtually the same as the 1989 particulars; in fact, apart from the different number of lots in which the estate was offered for sale, the particulars are virtually indistinguishable, and there was no public outcry in 1989. But in 1992 the wording of the sale particulars themselves can be seen to have added fuel to the fire. We have seen, at the beginning of this Chapter, how the particulars described the idyllic scenery. In 1989, the newspaper advertisement referred to the estate as being a '... paradise for those who love wilderness and abundant wildlife', and the word 'wilderness' was used in the description of the key features of the estate in the 1992 sale particulars. This is a description of the land which can be recognised and understood by people who see the Highlands as part of the dwindling resource of wild and desolate scenery in the British Isles, as a place where isolation and the absence of humans is to be treasured. But, of course, it is a description which by its emphasis on the unspoilt wilderness can be said to ignore, or at least put on one side, the fact that people work on the land in this wilderness and that before the clearances and emigrations of the late eighteenth and nineteenth centuries, many more people had occupied the land. Wilderness is not the natural state of the Highlands and Islands and we see this and the deep concern at the rural depopulation caused by the clearances, migrations and emigrations, reflected by the Gaelic poets. William Livingstone from Islay believed that wilderness was totally unacceptable.[22] See, for example, the powerful imagery in the last verse of his poem, *Fios chun a' Bhàird* (A message for the Poet) first published in 1863:

> *The beggar will not find shelter*
> *nor will the traveller get rest from his weariness,*
> *nor will a gospel preacher find an audience;*
> *injustice, foreigners and taxes have triumphed;*
> *the speckled adder is lying in coils*
> *on the floors where once there grew*
> *the big men that I saw there;*
> *take this message to the Poet.*[23]

The human desolation thus described is stark, particularly when contrasted with the first part of the poem which, in a disarming fashion describes a peaceful yet teeming life of the countryside before the clearances.[24] "Today we may feel that the poets tended to harp on the same tune for too long and in too elegiac manner, but we make such judgment in the light of a depopulated Highlands to which we have become accustomed. We are probably more willing to accept the Highlands as a 'wilderness' than were our nineteenth century poets."[25] But not too accustomed or indeed, willing. James Hunter has a vision of the glens being repopulated in a sensitive way.[26] In the BBC Landward programme 'Lights in the Glen', Eric Robson asked James Hunter: "But if the clearances are to be reversed, the glens repopulated and new communities created in Scotland's empty places, won't this intrude on what many wish to protect - the spirit of a precious wilderness?" Hunter replied: "The typical empty Highland glen with its treeless hillsides and its bare moorland is no more natural than a motorway embankment. It is something that has been created by what has been done to it by mankind over the last two, three, four hundred years … it has been made the way it is by people maltreating the land, by removing human communities. So let us have no talk of 'wilderness', let us talk about how we put back this landscape to the shape it ought naturally to be. For over a hundred years now in the Highlands and Islands we have seen the lights going out in glen after glen, in community after community. I think in the next hundred years we will see them coming back."[27] That wilderness is not the natural state has also been stated by the SCU and the RSPB: "The Wilderness Fallacy - Many parts of the Highlands and Islands have been described, from time to time, as wilderness. This is unscientific. Almost every landscape in northern Scotland bears the mark of human influence. Many of the most unpopulated localities were once thickly peopled - their populations having been expelled forcibly by the landlords responsible for the Highland Clearances. Crofters still aspire to win back these lost lands. There is no environmental reason why a measure of resettlement should not occur. Indeed there would be every reason to welcome reforms which made it possible to combine an element of resettlement with, for example, woodland regeneration and other measures designed to rehabilitate habitats which have been seriously degraded in the period since the Clearances."[28]

And so it is not difficult to understand the deep seated emotions which were aroused when the sale particulars described the estate as being a wilderness and when they said: "One need only enter Assynt to see the great sphinx-like mass of Suilven to sense the atmosphere of unreality, almost fantasy, which permeates even the character of the people who live there. Mountains such as Quinag, Canisp, Ben More Assynt, Cul Mor, Cul Beag, Stack Polly and Conival have the immense power to impress, and to serve to emphasise that man himself is perhaps the alien in this landscape." The particulars went on to say that

"... perhaps one of the most significant historical events in Assynt was the final arrest of the Marquess of Montrose at Ardvreck Castle ... beside Loch Assynt. This event effectively marked the end of the Civil War in Scotland in the mid 17th century." Now, even if one accepts the historical accuracy of this statement (there are, perhaps, some who would regard the Clashmore land raids in 1887 - certainly in the context of this story - as being more significant), one can understand how a combination of all these descriptions when coupled with a perfunctory reference to crofting on the estate, might not be taken too kindly by the crofting community; why such a description of the North Lochinver Estate in the sale particulars, and especially the use of the words 'wilderness' and 'alien', was regarded, in the words of Bill Ritchie, as 'offensive'. There can be little doubt that it strengthened the resolve of the crofters.

• The Assynt Branch of the SCU meets •

A special meeting of the Assynt Branch of the SCU was called for the 6th June to discuss the proposed sale of the estate. The importance of the meeting was clear; the notices for the meeting said: "As the sale will affect all of the townships from Achmelvich to Drumbeg all union members are urged to attend." The objective - to prevent the estate being broken up - was clear, but the answer to the question as to how this was to be achieved was not so obvious; but it became apparent that there was no real way to prevent the fragmentation of the estate without a sensible alternative being proposed. And so a two-fold strategy emerged: to discourage, or put off, other potential purchasers, but at the same time to offer a fair price for the land (insofar as such a price could be said to be 'fair' after a campaign to drive away the competition!)

An informal steering group was formed consisting principally of the three office bearers of the Assynt Branch of the SCU with Bill Ritchie as the acting secretary, Allan MacRae as the chairman and John MacKenzie as the vice chairman. In addition, each township was invited to nominate a member of the committee and the members were largely the grazings clerks, but not exclusively so. The members were: Felicite Basu from Clachtoll, John Blunt from Nedd, Donald King from Clashnessie, Aileen Kinnaird from Achnacarnin, Hughie Matheson from Drumbeg, Donald MacKenzie from Culkein Stoer, Ishbel MacAuley from Stoer, Derek MacLeod from Torbreck, Ian MacLeod from Achmelvich, Alastair MacIntyre from Balchladich and Pat MacPhail from Clashmore. The next step was to seek a mandate from the community to pursue the strategy and to take it forward as a community project comprising all the crofters on the estate, rather than as an SCU branch project.

On the 9th June 1992, following the initial meeting of the Assynt Branch of the SCU, a press release was issued by the Branch. This was a defining moment in the campaign. It set out the strategy and made clear the determination of the crofters (although at this stage there had not yet been a public meeting of the crofters.) It is worth quoting the press release in full:

"North Crofters to Fight Break-up of Croft Lands.

Crofters in Assynt, North West Sutherland expressed their anger and determination to resist the attempted sale in small lots of part of the former Assynt estate. The estate was sold by the Vesteys three years ago to a foreign-owned Company set up to trade in Scottish land. The Company, SPS Ltd, is now in the hands of the receiver and the croft land is to be sold by selling agents John Clegg and Co of Edinburgh, in small lots.

The crofters were told that this would cause administrative chaos with multiple land ownership. In some cases crofters would be paying rent on their inbye land to one landlord, rent for part of their grazing to another and rent for the remainder to yet another. Some crofters described as 'outrageous' the fact that if a crofter wanted to assign his croft to his son he would need the written permission of the new landowner even if he was a Surrey bank clerk.

The crofters are determined to put a halt to the increase in the fragmentation of croft lands at the hands of land speculators.

Among the options discussed was a programme of planned apportionments followed by applications to purchase the land under the terms of the Crofting Acts, which enables a crofter to buy the land at a fixed price. The crofters were told that this would result in the new landowner having to sell the land at well below the purchase price resulting in substantial financial losses to the speculators. Some of the crofters claim that the selling agents are being less than honest by not describing the implications of the fact that the land offered for sale is almost wholly croft land subject to the Crofting Acts.

The crofters agreed to pursue the possibility of establishing a Trust to purchase the land and are contacting a number of interested groups. They are also to seek an urgent meeting with the selling agent and receiver to make clear the implication of the sale so that prospective purchasers are fully aware of these.

Chairman Allan MacRae said that the crofters are looking to the Government agencies and local authorities in the Highlands and Islands to seize this opportunity to demonstrate their concern and support for crofting."

The concern at fragmentation of the croft lands and a possible multiplicity of landlords was made clear. So also was the intention to form a body which would offer to buy the land on behalf of the crofters. But the press release also mentioned the fact that the majority of the estate was croft land and referred to the possibility of a programme of planned apportionments of the common grazings followed by application to purchase under the right to buy provisions contained in the Crofting Reform (Scotland) Act 1976. This was important, because it was the start of the strategy to discourage other potential purchasers. The strategy was simple in its public message: "If you buy the estate and pay the full market price for it, you should do so in the clear understanding that we will use our rights to buy our crofts under the crofting legislation at a very low price leaving you with the bare bones of the land. These are croft lands. All you will have is the title and certain rights. You will be in conflict with the crofters." There were, as we shall see, difficulties involved in such a strategy, but there can be very little doubt that the threat to use the legislation in this way did keep away other potential purchasers.

The press release also marked another important element in the strategy: the start of the campaign, to be conducted through the media, to make clear the determination of the crofters to discourage other potential purchasers and to secure the support of the public, both moral and financial. The crofters were remarkably successful in their media campaign. The media reporting of the campaign was almost wholly sympathetic to the crofters and Ritchie is in no doubt that it was vital to the eventual success of the campaign. The steering committee worked closely with a number of journalists and made important use of 'off the record' briefings. David Ross of *The Herald* and Ian MacDonald of *BBC (Highland)* were of crucial importance to the Trust in helping the steering group to map out its media strategy. We shall return to the media campaign in Chapter 4, not least because of the parallels which can be drawn with the role of the media, as it then was, in the Crofters' War of the 1880s.

The 9th June press release was sympathetically reported, with headlines such as 'Crofters Aim to Fight Break-up of Estate by Buying Own Land' in *The Herald*[29] and 'Crofters Foresee Land Split Causing Chaos' in the *Press and Journal*,[30] although *The Scotsman* struck a slightly different tone with its bye-line 'Crofting Land Not a Pig in a Poke, Say Sellers'.[31]

• The Whitbread case - even the most urbane of landlords are rattled •

Had it not been for the most opportune timing of a landmark case heard in the Land Court and then in the Court of Session - the Whitbread case,[32] the Assynt crofters could not have made nearly such effective use of their threat to put into effect the 1976 Act provisions. In all likelihood, in fact, such a threat would have been an empty one. The decision in the Whitbread case played, therefore, a very important part in the campaign (albeit a part which consisted more 'in terrorem' than in fact), and was much quoted in the media. What was the case all about?

When Archie MacLellan lost his job as an estate worker on the Kinlochewe Estate in Wester Ross, he and his wife moved into temporary accommodation in Kinlochewe belonging to a local crofter, Donald MacDonald, who offered to the MacLellan family a plot of land on his croft as a house site. MacDonald began to take the necessary procedures to sell the site to Archie MacLellan's son, Donald and to decroft that part of the croft. The landlord, the Whitbread Estate, asked under the 'clawback' provisions of the 1976 Act, for half the market value of the site and the parties went to the Land Court, which in November 1991 delivered the stunning decision that the 'clawback' provisions of the 1976 Act did not apply to the transaction. The 'clawback' provisions are described in the Appendix on page 209 but broadly, where the right to buy provisions are exercised, they assure for the landlord half the development value of the land on any further sale of that land within a five year period. The arguments of the Whitbread Estate were that the transaction involved, in effect, two parts. The first was the acquisition of part of the croft land by MacDonald under which the price to be paid to the landlord (on the basis of the fifteen times the annual rent formula) was £15. The second was the disposal of that land to Donald MacLellan, a disposal which, the Estate argued, was subject to the 'clawback', and because the market value of the site was £25,000, the Estate was entitled to receive £12,500. But the arguments of the crofter were that, in applying to the Land Court, the crofter was only seeking authority to acquire the site and that the Land Court had granted the authority. At this stage the crofter had not actually acquired the site. The only acquisition which occurred was the acquisition by Donald MacLellan, not by Donald MacDonald. The argument was that where a crofter applies to the Land Court for an order under what is now section 12(1) of the 1993 Consolidation Act, authorising him to acquire croft land and under what is now section 13(1) of the 1993 Consolidation Act, the Land Court requires the landlord to convey the land to the crofter's nominee (even where the nominee is an independent third party). There is a single transaction and there is no room in that transaction for a supposed separate disposal by the crofter to his nominee - a separate disposal to which the 'clawback' provisions could apply.

The Land Court preferred the arguments of the crofter as, also, did three Scottish law Lords in the Court of Session on 5th June 1992, only four days before the issue of the first press release of the Assynt crofters at the start of their campaign.

In giving the opinion of the Court Lord Murray said: "Counsel for the appellant [the Whitbread Estate] informed us that, before the Land Court's decision in this case, landlords and crofters had generally interpreted the provisions in the sense for which the appellants had argued. The Land Court's decision had driven a coach and four through that consensus. Be that as it may, we have come to the conclusion that such a general understanding is not well-founded in law."[33] The position of landowners on the result of the case was voiced by John MacKenzie, the Chairman of the Highland Region branch of the Scottish Landowners Federation: "What is perfectly clear is that nobody thought that the law said what we now know it to say ... I don't think anybody thought that it was intended to say what the Court of Session says it says. So, if you get into a position where the law doesn't even say what people thought it did or even it was intended to say, it would be hardly surprising if we didn't contemplate trying to get that changed."[34] As Eric Robson said in the BBC Landward programme, 'Lights in the Glen': "Even the most urbane of landlords are rattled." [35]

The Whitbread case was important in two respects. It meant that the crofter could purchase all or part of his croft land from the landlord for a, usually, small sum and could sell it to a third party (not being a member of the crofter's family) without having to surrender any part of the market value to the landlord. But the real significance of the case from the point of view of the Assynt Crofters' Trust was that the case was taken to mean that a group of crofters could, without the 'clawback' provisions operating, join together and nominate a new landlord for their croft lands and remain as crofting tenants under the crofting legislation. In other words to maintain the status quo but as tenants of their own chosen landlord.

It is fortunate that the Assynt crofters did not actually have to put into effect a concerted plan to use the buy out provisions of the legislation in this way because a number of difficulties would have presented themselves. Difficulties would arise where the inbye land of each croft does not adjoin the common grazings and the interpretation of which common grazings are 'adjacent' to the croft could also raise difficult questions. Non-apportioned grazings cannot, of course, be bought under the provisions and if any significant part of the common grazings could not be apportioned the threat of a community buy out would be seen to be somewhat hollow, given that the interest of the purchaser would almost certainly be in the common grazings for their sporting value; so unless all or most of the common grazings could be brought under the provisions there would not be a substantial reduction in the value of the estate. Consideration would also have to be given as to how the croft dwelling houses would be dealt with. The original landlord would still retain the mineral and fishing rights, probably the foreshore where the land adjoins the sea, and a leaseback of the sporting rights.[36] Furthermore it is still possible that the 'clawback' provisions would still operate on a sale by the new landlord within the five year period which could inhibit development opportunities during those first five years. As not all the estate assets would be in the hands of the new landlord and because each individual crofter would (subject to what is said below) retain his right to purchase under the buy out provisions, which could result in a steady erosion of the community asset, funding opportunities might also be restricted.[37] Furthermore, a landlord presented with an effective community buy out would almost certainly argue (as he would be entitled under the legislation to do) that approval by the Land Court would cause hardship or be detrimental to the sound management of the estate; the Land Court is mainly concerned here with financial hardship to the landlord and it will rarely be the case that the estate in question will be the only source of the landlord's income and assets. However in a liquidation, such as was the case in Assynt, the liquidator might well have been able to claim financial hardship. Finally, and perhaps most significantly, it was not thought, at the time, wholly without doubt that the Whitbread decision really did mean that the crofter could nominate a new landlord and remain as a crofting tenant of the land. The alternative view of the case was that the crofter lost his tenancy rights when the land has been conveyed to the nominee.

However, the fact remains that where, in the absence of agreement with the landlord as to a purchase of the superior title, a well organised group of crofters makes use of the buy out provisions by nominating a Trust or similar vehicle to take the title (and assuming the crofters can remain as crofting tenants of the land), a landlord could well be left with having lost, for an insignificant sum, the title to a significant part of his land (for which he may well have paid a very significant sum) and be left with an unmarketable remnant. Faced with such a prospect the landlord may well wish to negotiate with the crofters rather than see the land being seriously devalued. This is just what happened in Assynt.

• The crofters meet to decide their strategy •

Following the issue of the 9th June press release, a public meeting of the crofters in the thirteen North Lochinver Estate townships was called for the evening of 20th June. The agenda for the meeting was the consideration of further proposals to safeguard the croft lands offered for sale in the townships and the support of moves to prevent the croft lands from being broken up and sold to land speculators. The crofters at the meeting were told that legal advice had been received on the setting up of a Crofters' Trust and that support in principle had been received from public agencies. The crofters were asked to show their commitment and were told that this was an exciting opportunity for the crofters of Assynt to lead the way towards a new era in land ownership. The meeting was highly charged with an obvious air of excitement. But there was also a degree of uncertainty at the meeting as to what the future would hold. There was a feeling that while the original landlord may not have been ideal, it was better than the threatened multiplicity. The meeting was, however, clear in its determination to ensure that the difficulties which fragmentation would cause should be made public. There was, not surprisingly, a degree of scepticsm that sufficient money could be raised to buy the estate. But those present at the meeting left little room for doubt as to their determination to succeed. As Bill Ritchie put it: "If we fail [with a just offer] we are determined ... to take the title to our land through the land courts against these foreign speculators."

The steering committee was given a mandate for the strategy and detailed planning had now to take place, and so before continuing with the story, we shall look, in the following paragraphs, at what this planning involved: the vehicle to be used to take the title to the land on behalf of the crofters, the sources of funding for the proposed purchase and the feasibility study and business plan for the project.

• The vehicle to be used for
community ownership •

Professional advice was clearly going to be important, and Bill Ritchie turned to Simon Fraser, a partner in the Stornoway firm of solicitors Anderson, MacArthur & Co. Simon Fraser, a well known and respected lawyer specialising in croft law had acted for both crofters and landlords (he was the factor to a number of estates) and was himself a crofter. But also, importantly, Simon Fraser had been one of the research team set up by the Arkleton Trust in 1990 to submit a report to the Highlands and Islands Development Board and the Scottish Crofters' Union on the legal and practical implications of a transfer of the Secretary of State for Scotland's crofting estates on Skye and Raasay to community ownership in response to the Government's Consultation Paper published on the subject.[38] The report was published on 6th June 1990 and recommended that if community ownership was to proceed, the most appropriate vehicle was a Company limited by guarantee. A significant amount of work had, therefore, already been carried out as to how a crofting estate might be transferred into community ownership.

The basic requirement was for a body to take the title to the land, a body which was to be controlled by, and operated in the interests of, the crofters of the North Lochinver Estate and the criteria for such a body were that it must be able to:

- own the estate as landlord, thus ensuring that the crofters could continue as crofting tenants
- be controlled entirely by the crofters and not be liable in any way to be taken out of their control
- raise finance by loan, grant or donation and to be able also to borrow and give security for such borrowings

- be responsive to the needs of the community
- initiate or take a direct hand in development
  opportunities on the estate

The three options examined were a Company limited by shares (either public or private), a Trust and a Company limited by guarantee.

The original favoured option was the Company limited by shares because at the start of the campaign it appeared that, apart from contributions from the crofters themselves, the most likely source of funding would be raising funds on commercial or near commercial terms, possibly through an issue of preference shares. However, as we shall see, it became clear at a relatively early stage that there was going to be a substantial number of non-crofters who were prepared to contribute to the campaign without necessarily having the motive of seeking a return. This meant that it would not be necessary to have a Company with a share capital with the controlling ordinary shares being held by the crofters and with the non-crofting contributors receiving preference, or at least non equity, shares. This was crucial because fund raising by the issue of shares would have involved compliance with corporate and financial services legislation which would have been burdensome, costly and time consuming.

A Trust was considered, but there were difficulties with this. To ensure control remained at all times with the crofters, the trustees would have to be drawn from the body of the crofters, but this could mean that there was no separation between the landlord (i.e. the trustees) on the one hand and the crofters on the other. While it is possible that using mechanisms such as a corporate trustee might have avoided this, it would have been complicated and, in any event, it was important that the crofters' position as crofting tenants would not be prejudiced in any way. If, of course, the trustees were not drawn from the crofters, then the crofters would not have been in effective control.

And so the third option of a Company limited by guarantee was used. This was a Company incorporated under the Companies Acts but where the liability of the members of the Company is limited, not by shares, but by the amount which each member undertakes (guarantees) to pay in the event of a winding up of the Company. There is, therefore, no share capital but there is still a body of members. This option would ensure that there was:

- membership and participation in decision making by all the crofters
- a suitable framework to ensure effective control by the crofters
- flexibility and control over changes in membership
- preservation of the estate as a community asset in perpetuity. It might be noted in this context that a Company limited by guarantee is probably a better vehicle than a Company limited by shares. With a Company limited by shares, each crofter would own shares which, without carefully drafted controls through a shareholders' agreement and the articles of association, could easily be sold to a third party. The Glendale estate in Skye which was bought by the crofters is an example of this. "Many of the crofts on the estate have now been sold on the open market. The communal framework for decision making has been virtually destroyed."[39]

And so a Company limited by guarantee with the name Assynt Crofters' Trust Limited was set up with the following objectives:

'- to raise funds by way of donation by the crofters and their friends, and grant to purchase our land and other resources in the North Lochinver Estate

- to improve the social, educational and cultural environment of the crofting communities and of the natural environment of Assynt, Sutherland

- to help fund viable investment and to secure property development and its management and to secure land renewal, and environmental and improvement projects for the crofting communities

- if we are successful, 100 per cent. of the development value will be retained locally for re-investment instead of 50 per cent. being extracted by absentee landlords.

- we can create affordable house sites for our local young people

- we can embark on woodland and other management projects creating some part-time employment

- we will create an atmosphere of optimism and opportunity and may be able to help our young people stay in their own communities and develop economic opportunities'[40]

We shall see later how these objectives closely reflect the benefits which the feasibility study and business plan would outline, and how they formed the main public arguments for support for the project, in particular in letters written by Bill Ritchie to opinion formers, in the Trust's communications with the media, and in the letter appealing for funds from the public. We should also note how a campaign which began with the idea of community ownership being embraced on a purely defensive basis - the objections to the fragmentation of the estate - had now taken on a much more positive note.

Membership of the Company was limited to the registered tenants of crofts within the estate, to owner-occupiers with a share in common grazings within the estate and to registered sub-tenants of such holdings. Each township could elect a Director to represent the township and each member had the right to nominate a person to serve as a Director for the township, and township nominations were decided on the basis of a simple majority. Recognising that it might not always be possible for a township to put forward a nominee from the township, it was agreed that a township could propose a person who lived outside the township, provided he or she fulfilled all the other qualifications. (Since the purchase, this has, however, changed. It is no longer a requirement that each township is represented. The Trust has experienced difficulties in attendance levels of township representatives and it was felt that appointments made on a simple majority within the Trust would achieve better representation.)[41] The qualification to be a Director was membership of the Company and being resident on the estate (although there is also provision for the co-option of Directors with special expertise which may be of value to the Trust; this provision would also enable non-crofting community involvement in the Trust (see Chapter 5). There would be provision for the retirement of Directors by rotation so that each Director served only three years.

• The sources of funding •

There were three principal costs which required funding. The legal and other professional costs, the cost of a feasibility study and business plan and, of course, the purchase price of the estate.

The immediate need was to be able to instruct lawyers and accountants to take forward the professional planning for the bid. Given that the original initiative for the buy-out

had come, essentially, from a branch of the Scottish Crofters'
Union, the Assynt Branch, the Union was an obvious
candidate as a provider of funds, and the Assynt crofters
were supported by an immediate promise of assistance from
the Union, which agreed to contribute £400 towards legal
fees. The Union also agreed to provide further funds up to
£1,000 towards the cost of establishing the necessary
business plan. The provision of such assistance was unusual
for the Union but was considered justified given the
'... enormous potential of the Lochinver case'. The Highland
Fund Foundation, an independent financial institution
formed in 1953 to provide the means of supplying crofters
and others with low interest rate loans for development
purposes, whose chairman Calum Bannerman had
unbounded enthusiasm for what the Assynt crofters were
doing, was true to its motto, *Caraid nan Gaidheal* (Friend of
the Gael), and agreed to give a grant of £3,000 towards the
legal and other professional costs to be incurred by the
Assynt crofters. Caithness and Sutherland Enterprise
(CASE) also offered immediate support of half of the cost of
preparing a business plan and economic statement, up to a
maximum amount of £1,500, and half of the cost of legal
fees and the associated costs of setting up a Company, up to
a maximum amount of £500. Andrew Thin, the Chief
Executive of CASE said: "For CASE the number one
priority is for the crofters to buy and control the land. I
regard it as very important that the hill as well as the inbye
comes into crofter ownership so that the full development
potential can be realised. Acquisition of the sporting rights
would be the icing on the cake, but it will be very difficult.
We have along with the Scottish Crofters Union, funded the
legal costs and the business plan. Further involvement will,
of course, depend on the outcome of the business plan."[42]

This assistance allowed the crofters to instruct the lawyers and accountants they needed and in particular, to draw up the feasibility study and business plan which would form the basis of the approach to be made to public and other bodies for funds to meet the purchase price of the estate. As we shall see later, the feasibility study and business plan also gave the crofters the assurance they needed that a purchase of the estate was an economic proposition.

But the bulk of the funding was, of course, required to pay for the estate. As we have seen, it was the intention of the crofters to pay a fair price for the land, but not an inflated price. Bill Ritchie made clear the principles on which a bid would be made at the public meeting of the crofters on the 20th June: "What we are planning to do is to first of all buy the North Lochinver Estate by offering a fair price, and I emphasise the fair price. We are not in the market for getting millions like the foreign operators. We have to stake our just claim and make a just offer for our assets."

Professional valuations and the feasibility study and business plan would show what a fair price was, but, with the sale particulars showing a guide price of £473,000, the crofters were clearly going to have to raise funds of hundreds of thousands of pounds. This was a daunting prospect. Allan MacRae put it like this to the crofters, in words for public consumption: "We can't win on our own. We simply don't have the resources to raise the money among ourselves. But we are going to raise as much as we can and we would certainly hope that all the other bodies who are saying they are so concerned about the land up here are going to support us. The opportunity is there. It is now for them to show that kind words are not good enough. They have got to back it up with something and we are giving them the opportunity."

The first element in the fund raising plans involved the crofters themselves. This was never going to produce very significant sums, as Allan MacRae had said, but it was vital that the crofters should be seen seriously to be putting their own money towards the project, both psychologically for themselves, to prove their own determination, but also as a sign to the public and other bodies of their own commitment. As Allan MacRae said to the crofters at the meeting on 20th June: "So really, it is up to us. Basically, to begin with I believe that once we get some money together then the support will come to us. I am sure of this. But we must show we mean business. It is not going to happen. We have got to make it happen. And it starts right with us." Bill Ritchie wrote to all the crofters telling them that, as a group, they should aim to raise, from the public, £80,000 with a challenge for each crofting family to raise £1,000.[43] The figure of £80,000 had a real significance. £40,000 represented the value of the estate on the basis of the right to buy provisions of the crofting legislation and the steering group considered that a figure of twice this sum was the 'correct' sum to be aimed at by the crofters themselves.

The second element involved the public. There was a sense that members of the public might want to contribute to the project. Initially it was thought, as has been mentioned, that these contributions might come by means of a non-voting preference share issue, but as was discussed above, the legal and technical issues were to prove too burdensome and expensive. At a very early stage, there was a suggestion, albeit perhaps in jest, that one of the small islands forming part of the estate could be offered as a 'prize' to the first investors. In the event, however, people appeared to be willing to contribute funds without requiring anything in return apart from the knowledge that they were, in some way, involved in, and part of, a defining moment in Highland history. However the steering group was anxious that members of the public who wanted to contribute significant sums should be able to have something tangible to show that they were involved, to allow them to feel they were part of the process, and so honorary membership of the Trust was offered to all those who contributed £500 or more and a handsome certificate was to be issued in due course (see page 105). It was originally also hoped that tax relief would be available through Gift Aid for contributions, but this proved not to be possible given the difficulty in meeting the necessary pre conditions - the relief of poverty, education etc.

Significant support from the public would, of course, require a public campaign, putting forward the objectives of the Trust. The press and the media generally played a very important part, but they did so because the steering group communicated very effectively the message of what the Trust was trying to do, with an unashamed appeal to the emotions. Bill Ritchie wrote a number of letters to opinion formers such as the local M.P. Robert Maclennan, the chairman of the Scottish Conservative party, the Crofters Commission and the CBI. Ritchie described the background to the present situation and expressed his concern that unless the selling agents were convinced by someone other than the crofters of the merits of their case, they would not allow the crofters sufficient time to put their plans into effect. There appeared to be a real worry on the part of the steering group that the crofters would not be allowed to compete on equal terms; one of the early letters from the Trust to the selling agents asked for a confirmation that other offers would be made in the knowledge of the Trust's intentions, if necessary, to acquire the land under the right to buy provisions in the crofting legislation, "... to ensure we are competing on even terms."[44] There was even a suggestion at one stage that 'anti-crofter forces' had delayed the eventual success of the Trust, with rumours of a possible link between the former estate owner, Edmund Vestey and the selling agents.[45] It may be that this paranoia is explained by the antipathy there still seems to exist between crofters and landlords. Tom Morton writing in *The Scotsman*[46] said: "Conspiracy theories breed easily in places like Assynt, barely a generation away from the last survivors of the clearances." Auslan Cramb believes that over the last 60 years, the relationship in Assynt between landlord and community has deteriorated to such an extent that it is irreparable.[47] Allan MacRae believes that Highlanders still grow up with an anti-landlordism feeling because of history, although he would be quick to admit that not all landlords are, by definition, bad. However, "Highland people have long memories - there is no doubt about that" is how he put it in the television programme, 'Lights in the Glen'.[48] In any event, there was clearly still some bad feeling between crofter and landlord. In August, Bill Ritchie wrote to Edmund Vestey expressing his concern at the consequences which flowed from Mr Vestey's decision to sell the croft lands in 1989 to a foreign property Company and the subsequent bankruptcy of that Company. He ended the letter by saying: "I would welcome the opportunity to meet with you and discuss our plans for the croft lands. You may feel able to lend your support to our initiative." No such meeting took place and, as we shall see, there continued to exist an undercurrent of antipathy. In the event, Simon Fraser recalled that the negotiations and dealings between the Trust and the selling agents were straightforward and business like.

Bill Ritchie outlined the objectives of the Trust in these letters as follows:

- to put an end to the stranglehold of absentee landlordism
- to retain 100 per cent. of development value locally for re-investment

- to create affordable housing sites for local young people "... instead of landlords demanding huge payments for the title to house sites on our own land from our own families"
- to pursue woodland and other management projects.

He made the point that the crofters now had the mechanism to do all of this "... without destroying the security of tenure and sense of community which the vast majority of crofters showed they would not give up for owner occupancy unless encouraged to do so under the right to buy provisions of the crofting legislation," a reference to the Whitbread decision. He ended these letters with an appeal for help and support and with the stirring words: "We have history, morality and the law on our side. And we are determined."[49]

The public appeal was launched at a meeting in Stoer School on 28th July 1992. This was a seminal moment in the campaign. The chosen venue for the meeting had been the community hall in Stoer but as the hall became more and more crowded, it became obvious that it was far too small to allow for everyone who wanted to be present to participate; there were people outside the hall who could not find room within. Over 120 people wanted to be part of this historic gathering. So the meeting was moved to the general purposes room in Stoer School and, even there, the room was packed with people sitting on the window sills and standing in the aisles. It was a dramatic, and moving, demonstration of support and enthusiasm. In the press release announcing the meeting, Allan MacRae said, in one of his challenging statements, that he was "confident that the agencies would support the crofters and help put into action their declared policies for the first time. Together with the Assynt crofters they could take crofting forward into the 21st century - they should not miss this opportunity." The release said that at the meeting on 28th July, the crofters would outline their proposals and call for support from throughout the Highlands and Islands. Bill Ritchie and Allan MacRae outlined the progress the Trust had made thus far; in particular the support the Trust had received from the agencies. Ritchie was clear in his message to the meeting: the intention was "... to wrest control of our land from the foreign landowners [who had] neither understanding or care for our history or future."[50] So far as the appeal to the public was concerned, Bill Ritchie said that no special favours could be offered to donors: "The most we can offer you is a place in history if we succeed."[51] The public appeal letter (see page 102 & 103) promised donors that their names would be inscribed on a roll of honour and referred to the offer of honorary membership of the Trust for those who donated more than £500.[52] The public appeal letter set out the objectives of the Trust in the terms set out on pages 38 and 39 and ended with the familiar and stirring (but curiously slightly altered) words: "We have history, justice and the law on our side. With help from our friends we will succeed."

The launch of the public appeal was widely and strongly publicised in the press with headlines such as: 'Assynt Estate 'land for the people' Fund is Launched',[53] 'Crofters' Historic Move Achieves Lift-Off',[54] 'Highlanders Fight to Halt Laird's Clearance Sale',[55] 'Crofters Act Together To Buy Estate',[56] 'Packed Rally Starts Assynt Appeal',[57] 'Crofters Launch Bid to Buy £473,000 Estate',[58] and 'Highland Battle Begins'.[59]

The public appeal raised, through donations and pledges, somewhat in excess of £130,000 from 824 people. The sums received varied from postage stamps and postal orders to thousands of pounds, from the South of England to the North of Scotland, from over three hundred different towns and villages in Scotland, England and Wales, and from abroad. Letters of support, donations and pledges were received from old people with shaky hands, with messages such as: 'my grandfather was cleared - you've got to do this', from people who had enjoyed holidays in Assynt as children, from people who had read about the Assynt crofters in the newspapers, from public figures, for example, European M.P. Winnie Ewing and M.Ps Charles Kennedy, Ray Michie and Alex Salmond gave their support and the local M.P. Robert Maclennan publicly made a gift of £1300 at the meeting on 28th July, £50 for every year he had served as M.P, speaking movingly of the clearance of his forbears from the Ullapool area. The Gaelic rock band Runrig also gave generously, as did the *West Highland Free Press* with a pledge of £1,000. The appeal fired the imagination of a substantial number of people in a way which might, at first sight, have seemed surprising, but in retrospect could be seen as a recognition of a number of different emotions; support for the little man against the rich and famous; love of the Highlands and the Highland way of life, and from the Highland diaspora in the Lowlands, cities and overseas a recognition that this was the realisation of what the crofters had been fighting for from the 1880s, the return of the land to the people. The one disappointing note was the relatively low level of support from abroad, given the strength of the Highland diaspora overseas and the historic reasons for such a diaspora - in particular the clearances and emigrations of the late eighteenth century and the nineteenth century. There had been a lively international response to the requests for help for the Highlands after the famine year of 1846, from, in particular, Scottish expatriates in Canada, India and the East Indies.[60] It might have been expected that there would have been an encouraging response from the Highland diaspora overseas. However, as Bill Ritchie admits, the fact that there was not may be explained by the fact that not enough work was put into an international appeal, in particular to the Clan societies in Canada, New Zealand and Australia. But given the burden of work which the steering group had and the very short time which was available before the closing date for offers, this is hardly surprising and the degree of success achieved at home is a tribute to the overall success of the public appeal. In the event, funds were received from New Zealand, Canada, The United States, Germany, France, Italy, Brazil, South Africa and Zimbabwe.

The third element involved various public bodies, but before turning to an examination of this element, the most important in terms of the amount of funds raised overall, it is worth noting that the steering group also considered, in the early days, the possibility of raising funds from other bodies such as the John Muir Trust, the RSPB and the World Wildlife Fund for Nature. The John Muir Trust, a charitable Trust with environmental aims, was working in partnership with people who earned their living from the land and it was in a land purchase phase. So far as the RSPB was concerned, it was thought that the move by the Assynt crofters to acquire control over their own resources was in line with the thinking in the joint paper produced by the RSPB and the Scottish Crofters' Union on the future of crofting and the environment[61] which had just been published. Letters written by Bill Ritchie to each of these organisations show that a number of the Assynt crofters had environmental considerations in mind in relation to the development of the estate and that they were also aware of the drawbacks to development of the natural resources of the land by the crofters as tenants (touched on in the Appendix) - "We will be able to look at the overall management of our resources, especially the land, in light of new opportunities not only for economic development but also for land management which is sensitive to the wildlife and landscape interest ... with the new opportunities for woodland planting and especially native woodland regeneration opened up by the Crofting Forestry Act it is perfectly appropriate that the crofters should acquire the landowning title as the permission of the landowner is a prerequisite for new woodland planting. Assynt has a number of good semi-natural woodlands from which regeneration could be expanded as well as a number of other important wildlife features."[62]   The RSPB was interested in the proposal and keen to be involved with the Assynt Crofters' Trust, feeling that it would be very much a practical implementation of the ideas expressed in the joint RSPB/SCU paper. However, the RSPB would not have been able to gift any money to the Trust but would only have been able to commit funds under the terms of a management agreement regarding conservation management of the estate.

In the event, none of these possibilities was pursued, largely because the crofters did not wish to gain title to the land only to have their hands tied with regard to its use and development. The Trust was, however, to accept funds from Scottish Natural Heritage, but, as we shall see, not without a good deal of heart searching and debate.

As to the public bodies, there was early support given by Highland Regional Council. Bill Ritchie contacted HRC shortly after the decision to proceed was taken in principle and HRC was quoted in the press as being supportive: "Clearly, if the local crofters were to come up with economically viable plans, and show a strong unity of purpose by forming a Trust to take control of the situation, then I am sure the Council would want to look very seriously at ways in which we might be able to give assistance."[63] A formal application for a grant of £10,000 under the HRC

Community Development Projects Initiative was made on behalf of the Trust in August 1992 and, towards the end of September, HRC notified the Trust that a grant of £10,000 was agreed. Support also came from Highland District Council in the form of a £1,000 donation.

CASE considered the plans of the Assynt crofters to be a pilot scheme of considerable importance to their area and to the Highlands and Islands in general, and agreed, in the middle of September, a grant of £50,000 provided the Trust raised at least £80,000 from private sources. Iain Robertson, the HIE chief executive, said: "We are actively supporting this particular bid because it embraces the overall aim of the HIE network to allow the people of the area to realise their full potential through stimulating business development, strengthening the community and raising the quality of life."[64] Writing in *The Independent* shortly after the CASE grant was announced James Cusick raised a possibly worrying development: "... *The Independent* has learned that lawyers in Edinburgh acting for potential bidders are investigating possible legal action against HIE if their clients are outbid, over the validity of the HIE cash. Iain Robertson, HIE's chief executive, said he would "prefer not to consider the political aspects of the contribution, but we may have to." Commenting on the grant award, Mr Balfour [Robert Balfour of John Clegg & Co, the Seller's agents] described the HIE's decision as 'odd'."[65] However, nothing further was heard of this. No doubt it was not only the crofters who were making use of the media to attempt to influence events.

The largest single contribution to the project came from Highland Prospect Limited, the investment company established by Highland Regional Council and which provided grants and soft loans for small businesses. In fact, it was the first financial assistance towards the purchase price received from the public sector. Announced on 20th August,

1992, it marked a very significant development because the assistance came in the form, not of a grant, but of a secured loan of £90,000. Of the seven lots in which the North Lochinver Estate was offered for sale, lot 1 was the Torbreck Estate, comprising 10,056 acres. Within the lot was Torbreck Lodge. In financial terms, Torbreck Lodge was probably the most valuable part of the whole estate and it was not, of course, part of the croft lands. It was, however, a valuable asset; in many ways it was the jewel in the estate, all the rest being croft lands. There were 40 acres of woodland and the lodge, the former manse, had been modernised and refurbished in 1991 with outline planning permission for a new lodge, and the Manse Loch fishing system.[66] If the Trust had bid for the estate but without including Torbreck Lodge, the sums required would have been considerably less. But the steering group considered it to be important that their bid should not have any weaknesses in it. If they had excluded Torbreck Lodge, the sellers would, no doubt, have wanted to retain the sporting rights and there would almost certainly, have been a considerable debate over whether the Manse Loch fishing system should be included or excluded. These were issues which the steering group did not want to have to deal with and, in any event, if the Trust was to have control over the development of the estate assets, this was clearly an asset which could be developed or used to the benefit of the crofters. And so the strategy ultimately decided on was to bid for the whole estate (although, as we shall see, a very small part of the estate, lot 3, being the cottage at Clashmore, was not purchased) even though this would mean the Trust would be immediately in debt from the date of entry. We shall also see that at a late stage in the process the Trust came under some pressure to exclude the lodge and the fishing system from its bid. The loan of £90,000 was negotiated with Highland Prospect with an initial very low rate of interest which increased to a market rate if Torbreck Lodge was not sold within a year of purchase.

The application for financial assistance made by the steering group to Scottish Natural Heritage (SNH) was interesting for a number of reasons. SNH is a government body established: 'To secure the conservation and enhancement of Scotland's unique and precious natural heritage - the wildlife, habitats and landscapes through the long partnership between people and nature .... Our aim is to help enjoy Scotland's natural heritage responsibly, understand it more fully and use it wisely so that it can be sustained for future generations.' Bill Ritchie was a Board member of the North West Region of SNH and recognised at an early stage that SNH might consider providing financial assistance for the Assynt crofters. Writing at the beginning of July to Terry Keating at SNH in Golspie[67] Bill Ritchie explained the proposal of the crofters to buy the estate and set out the 'natural heritage' case that the crofters were keen to manage the resources in an environmentally sensitive way and that they would like help to assess the potential for environmental enhancement of the land, building on crofting practices. He explained that there was much degradation of both the hill and the inbye land and that the crofters wanted to explore ways in which this might be reversed either by building on traditional practices or by new land use initiatives like the extension of native woodlands. He wondered whether the Agricultural Working Group of the North West Region Board, which was looking at the possibility of setting up a number of pilot schemes intended to demonstrate good crofting practices and resource management, would consider the North Lochinver Estate as a suitable location. Keating replied in an encouraging manner. He confirmed that the crofters' interest in reversing degradation of both inbye and hill ground was an interest which SNH shared, and suggested a discussion. Ritchie also wrote to Sir John Lister-Kaye, the Chairman of the North West Board of SNH.[68] Sir John was clearly interested in helping the Assynt crofters. Speaking on the BBC Landward programme, 'Lights in the Glen',[69] he said: "Where it is perfectly possible and realistic to see clear environmental gain for the public good then there must be a case for financial assistance."

A formal application on behalf of the Trust was made in August and SNH confirmed, in early September, that a grant of up to £20,000 had been approved, but that the formal offer of grant would contain conditions specifically related to the Board management objectives of North Assynt in a way which would maintain and enhance the natural heritage value of the land, which derived in part from traditional crofting management in the area. It was the likelihood of conditions such as this which, of course, had caused the heart searching within the steering group as to whether or not an application should be made. The formal offer of a £20,000 grant[70] was made at the end of 1992. The offer required the Trust to include in its management objectives certain proposals for the sustainable use of the natural heritage.

The grant given by SNH raised interesting and difficult issues. It brought to the fore the whole question of the extent to which conservation bodies should be involved in land ownership.[71] It is probably fair to say that the decision as to whether or not to apply for the grant, and the terms on which it was to be accepted, caused as much discussion and debate among the Assynt crofters as any other issue during the campaign. And it would be wrong to disguise the fact that there was quite a serious difference of opinion between members of the steering group on the main issue: the extent to which outside bodies providing financial assistance to the Trust should be able to direct, control or have influence over the running of the estate by the crofters. The crofters were keyed up to become masters of their own land and of their own destiny and were reluctant to allow a dilution of that new found sovereignty. At the time the grant was announced by SNH in September 1992, this difference of opinion became public. Sir John Lister-Kaye said: "My Board has given its unanimous support to this grant aid which is intended to assist with the purchase of this land in order to encourage its environmentally sensitive management ... this area has outstanding natural heritage interest and if the croftlands do come into Trust ownership, then SNH will be advising on sustainable land management, native woodland regeneration, access provisions, and habitat and landscape enhancement projects. SNH will certainly need to discuss with the Trust how we can work in partnership to secure the best management for the estate which will take full account of its important natural heritage interests."[72] The press release issued by SNH also referred to the fact that the estate lay within the Assynt-Coigach National Scenic Area and that it had a Site of Special Scientific Interest (SSSI) at Ardvar (from where, of course, Allan MacRae's great grandfather was cleared). There were three National Nature Reserves as near neighbours and the press release said that the area had a high conservation value with significant bird and plant communities. The conservation case was, thus, strongly put. John MacKenzie, on behalf of the Trust and putting, as it were, the crofters' side, said: "Obviously I am delighted at this award which is a further confirmation of the public support for our efforts. It is also recognition of the past century and a half of environmentally sensitive husbandry which has left something worth conserving on Highland croftlands. This is in contrast to many of the areas that were cleared last century leaving the empty, unnatural

environment we can see today."[73] He also said: "Land use in
the context of crofting is intrinsically conservation-friendly.
This is demonstrated by the fact that, after generations of
crofting activity, there are to be found in Assynt nationally-
important numbers of rare species of birds and other
wildlife."[74]

Allan MacRae, however, was quoted in the press[75] as
saying that while he would be happy to be *advised* (emphasis
added) by organisations such as SNH, he would not wish to
compromise the Trust's own control over what was best for
the land. He noted SNH's intentions to work in partnership
with the crofters, but said: "We are very conscious of the
environment - crofters always have been. I hope they [SNH]
are giving in the same spirit as the public are donating, by
supporting the view that the people on the land up here are
the ones best qualified to manage it."[76] Judith Napier, writing
in the *Press & Journal* on the 15th September, said: "A grant
of up to £20,000 from Scottish Natural Heritage rang
warning bells among the crofting community, following
as it did SNH's controversial involvement with the
Forest Farm plantation. Trust steering group chairman Mr
Allan MacRae perceives that there has been perhaps too
little talk about the people and their crofting heritage, too
much about the 'wildlife paradise' tag with which the estate
was originally marketed. Adamant that neither management
agreements nor advice will compromise the crofters'
authority over their own land, he rejects 'capitalising' moves
by public agencies." Allan MacRae was quite clear in his
view as to who should manage the land: "It must be clearly
understood that what we are concerned with here is the
people who live and work in this community and, if the
bid is successful, we reserve the right to manage the land in
our own way - no one will be allowed to undermine the
integrity of that."[77] That this was not just a matter of

academic interest would become clear later, after the estate
was purchased by the Trust, when differences appeared to
arise between the Trust and SNH over the proposed
development of Loch Poll for a hydro-electric project (see
Chapter 3).

While this is not the place to discuss crofting and the
environment[78] (but we shall see in Chapter 3 how the Trust
is undertaking environmentally sensitive projects on the
estate), it might be worthwhile considering, in brief, what
might lie at the root of the sensitivities which undoubtedly
exist. We have seen how the commercial use by landowners
of land in the Highlands led to the clearances and to the
creation of the crofting community. Of how, in particular,
the coming of sheep in large numbers meant that the
Highlanders were moved to coastal areas where they were
expected to make a living as best they could from the small
lots of land made available, and from the sea. The
landowners also found they could exploit the timber
resources of their lands to meet the needs of the southern
industrial revolution. When the sheep became unprofitable
in the mid to late nineteenth century, the deer forest was
created as "... a cash bonanza for the lairds who were
downcast by the way the wool profits had so rapidly
evaporated."[79] This was a development which has been
described as inevitable.[80] The Highland sporting estate had
thus come into being. We saw, in Chapter 1, how this
affected the people. But it also had its effects on the land.
Before the sheep came, the Highland way of life, depending
as it did, on cattle rearing, seemed to provide a stable and
sustainable future for the environment. But the commercial
landlordism which developed at the end of the eighteenth
century and which brought the sheep, the destruction of
large swathes of native oak and pine forests and the vast
expansion of red deer numbers, can be said to have caused

a serious degradation of the Highlands because of the exclusively extractive nature of such land use.[81] Now, the topic of land use in the Highlands is a particularly sensitive one and there is often seen to be a conflict between growth and aesthetics, between those who advocate what might be described as the traditional land use i.e. land is a resource from which a living is made by farming, forestry and fishing, or by sporting or industrial use, and those who advocate a 'post romantic' land use i.e. for recreation, for the spiritual enjoyment of a wilderness area and as a refuge for wild life;[82] the private property versus heritage conflict. It is not necessarily the case that these uses are mutually irreconcilable, but in any event the crofter is often seen to be the enemy of the environmental or conservation lobby, "... both Highlanders and environmentalists having engaged in a good deal of mutual name-calling, not to say vilification."[83] This is probably unfair, and indeed, the joint document produced by the RSPB and the SCU[84] points this up and James Hunter believes it should be possible for the Highlands to be "... a living demonstration that community, culture and nature can, after all, be made compatible with one another."[85] However, it does no harm to remember that the way of life which the crofter has, and the current use of land in the Highlands might be argued to be the consequence of the commercial exploitation of the land by landlords going back into history. It was not the crofters who created this situation. Indeed, it could almost be said that it is the Government which has aggravated the problem through the type of public support which has been available to crofters.[86] If, then, there is a certain sensitivity amongst crofters at being told how the land should be used, this is perhaps understandable.

• The feasibility study and business plan •

The preparation of the feasibility study and business plan was of crucial importance. The crofters needed to know whether the purchase of the estate and community management of it was an ongoing economic proposition; as we have seen, they also needed a properly prepared case to present to the public bodies from whom funds were to be sought. The steering group asked Steve Westbrook, an economist from Nairn, and Graeme Scott of Angus MacKenzie & Co., chartered accountants in Inverness, to put together the necessary report. It was produced remarkably quickly.

It is worth considering the report in some detail, not merely because of its importance in confirming to the crofters that the purchase of the estate was an economic proposition and because it formed the basis of the Trust's grant applications, but because of what it tells us about the economics of a small Highland estate, particularly one which is predominantly a crofting estate with little sporting potential.

The basic economic reason for purchasing the land was to ensure that the income and wealth which the estate was capable of generating should be developed and that it should stay within the local community. As Bill Ritchie said in the BBC Landward programme: "We believe that there are new opportunities arising from the management of the land which are not necessarily traditional deer stalking, fishing or even sheep grazing. There are new opportunities arising and we as crofters want to be able to be part of these new opportunities."[87] The report recognised that many of the potential benefits could only be realised in the long term, and so the purchase was as much about providing for future generations as it was for improving the current position of the crofters. That there was potential for development had been noted by John MacEwan when he wrote in his seminal work, *Who Owns Scotland?* : "In 1970 I saw a good deal of Vestey's land; it is not all poor. The valuable Stoer section, for instance, was scandalously underdeveloped."[88]

The report summarised the economic and social benefits of purchasing the estate as follows:

- the psychological benefits derived from the crofters being in control of their own destiny. The point might also, of course, be made that the other side to this is that the crofters would have the burden of responsibility for the management of the estate and be involved in decision making at levels which they had not previously experienced, factors which had in the past discouraged crofters from becoming involved in managerial control of crofting lands

- population retention or growth and the generation of employment opportunities, generally of a part-time nature and thus compatible with other crofting activities - the traditional pattern, in fact, of croft employment. Information available from Highland Regional Council, estimated at the time the report was written, showed that overall in the last nine years, population had increased by some 8 per cent. in the three areas of Stoer, Drumbeg and Lochinver (the increase in Drumbeg broadly matching the decrease in Stoer).[89] While increasing employment opportunities in fish farming, fishing and tourism had encouraged a tendency for young people to stay in the local area, so far as the estate itself was concerned, the report considered that it had not been run with any obvious objective to create employment opportunities. One part time job was provided by the estate and the individual concerned lived outside the area. Furthermore, the availability of affordable housing was recognised as a constraint on population growth or, indeed, retention.[90] An estate housing policy could improve the supply of houses for young people and others on low incomes, could create employment opportunities in house building and maintenance and generate income through the sale of house plots. The regional office of Scottish Homes was very supportive of the principle of estate ownership by the crofters because land availability at reasonable prices had been a serious problem in the area. It was thought that under community ownership it would be easier than it had been in the past for new houses to be built. Overall, it was considered that, in the short term, ownership of the estate could generate at least ten additional full time equivalent jobs. These jobs would be mostly part time, providing income support for in the region of twenty families. While over fifty per cent. of Assynt sheep flocks numbered less than fifty sheep, sheep farming was still an important part of the crofters' incomes and the trends in the European Community support schemes which suggested that sheep may become less attractive as a basic source of income in the future, meant that there was an increasing requirement for new employment opportunities to be created and for other sources of croft income to be created. Community ownership of the estate could assist this.

- more control over community development, especially through the types of housing developed, the leasing policy over any housing for rent and through a more pro-active stance which could be taken with the Crofters Commission in relation to absentee crofters. This point highlights the difference of emphasis

between the approach which a landlord whose interests
in the estate are mainly sporting would be likely to
adopt and a landlord who is, in effect, a crofting
landlord. Under the Crofters Commission rules of
procedure to deal with absentee crofters, the
Commission asks the landlord for his observations on
whether it would be in the general interests of the
crofting community in the district that a croft should be
available for re-letting.[91] A crofting landlord supported
by the community might be expected to be more likely
to take a stronger position on re-letting than a landlord
who does not have the same interests. A past chairman
of the Crofters Commission, Archie Macleod, believed
that the initiative in Assynt was important in this
respect: "I think this is perhaps the beginning of
something really worthwhile in maintaining the whole
ethos of crofting. The danger always is losing crofts
from the crofting stock, and provided every care and
step is taken to ensure that the crofts won't slip easily
out of crofting into a free market, then I think the
Assynt initiative is commendable."[92]

- improved estate management, in terms of:
- farming practices
- natural woodland regeneration. The Crofters Forestry
  (Scotland) Act 1991 (see the Appendix), passed to
  enable crofters to use their land for 'forestry purpose', is
  defective in that schemes still require the specific
  consent of the landlord. Under community ownership
  this process would, thus, become much simpler. The
  report considered that on the North Lochinver Estate,
  natural regeneration was particularly appropriate and
  suggested that with the required training, a planting
  regime of some twenty years could support locally
  some 162 man years of work. The organisation of

forestry on an estate wide basis should allow economies in the potentially high costs of fencing and promote the integration of farming and sporting activity

- deer population control and enhancement, and sporting value. Contrary, perhaps, to the perception of other parties interested in purchasing the estate, the North Lochinver Estate was not a sporting estate in any economic sense. It is, of course, a fact that the sale particulars in both 1989 and 1992 had spoken of the salmon and sea trout fishing system on the estate and of deer stalking, particularly in relation to the Torbreck lot, but as an income producing asset on its own, the sporting potential was thought to be limited. The report estimated that deer stalking was, in reality, effectively limited to some eight stags a year and that the salmon and sea trout had not been present to any real degree in the rivers for a number of years. Enhancing the sporting prospects was not considered to be an economic proposition, although brown trout fishing was good and this had helpful implications for the development of tourism in the area

- attraction of tourists and other visitors. Rather than being a direct source of revenue, trout fishing on the estate lochs would more likely be of value to the area's accommodation business, including crofters with self-catering. Other tourist attractions such as wildlife tours, boat trips and sea angling could be provided by the Trust for the benefit of the community.

Finally, the report emphasised the benefits, to a large extent intangible, of community ownership, over and above the psychological benefits. Community ownership ought to promote cooperation between the crofters in relation to the development of the estate generally, the agreement on conservation measures and the provision of social and recreational facilities in the townships. A vision for the future: the management of land as an asset for the value and benefit not just of one person, the landlord, but of the community as a whole. There was no obvious commercial gold mine in the estate, but ownership and management of the estate by the crofters was a viable economic proposition. As has been stressed, the estate was basically a crofting estate, but such potential as it did have could be turned to the benefit of the community.

• The Assynt Crofters' Trust is set up •

We return now to the story of the purchase of the estate. Following the public meeting on the 20th June, Allan MacRae wrote to Simon Laird at John Clegg & Co requesting a meeting between representatives of the crofters and their legal adviser and the selling agents. He made it clear that the crofters were anxious to arrive at an amicable agreement and said that the public meeting of the crofters had given its unanimous agreement to set up the Trust to negotiate a purchase of the croft lands 'based on values defined by the Crofting Acts plus a sum for the sporting rights.'[93] At this stage, there was no firm view that the whole estate was to be purchased; certainly all the croft lands and the sporting rights would be bid for, but a decision as to whether the feuhold property should be included in the bid would await the feasibility study and business plan and, indeed, the discussions as to the level of funds which might sensibly be anticipated. Bill Ritchie did, however, recognise that the crofters might have to bid for the whole estate if the crofters were to succeed, particularly as it might be difficult to separate the feuhold and the croft lands. In his letter to Simon Laird, MacRae pointed out that if the crofters failed in their bid and if the croft lands were broken up, the crofters would prepare a co-ordinated plan to purchase the croft lands under the right to buy provisions of the Crofting Acts and, using the Whitbread decision, would nominate the Trust as the owner. The steering group clearly considered that it was important that the liquidator, and indeed any other prospective purchasers, should be in no doubt as to their intentions and Allan MacRae asked for Simon Laird's assurance that the liquidator was informed of them. The battle lines were thus clearly drawn at an early stage. If the crofters were not able, or allowed, to buy the estate (or at least the croft lands and sporting rights), they would take action to make it unlikely that anyone else would want to.

Simon Laird responded to MacRae's letter by saying that a closing date for the sale would be set shortly, but that the crofters would be kept fully informed. He also said that the sale particulars had been drawn up, and the estate lotted, to provide different sectors of the market, including the crofting communities, an opportunity to purchase. So far as a meeting was concerned, Laird thought that, at this stage, it might not be productive.

Simon Fraser was instructed immediately after the public meeting on 20th June to have a Company up and running by the 27th June, and Bill Ritchie arranged meetings for that week at the offices of Highland Regional Council in Inverness with Peter Peacock and his advisers and George Campbell and Derek Flyn from the SCU, to discuss fund-raising and the level of support which might come from the public bodies.

The crofters were given a progress report at the end of an important week at a meeting in Stoer in the evening of 27th June. The notice of the meeting said that Simon Fraser would explain the details of the setting up of the Trust and made the important point that the liability of each crofter would be limited to £1. The notice ended: "Although membership of the Trust will be voluntary we need all the crofters to join the Trust to show solidarity and to gain the wholehearted support of the agencies. Your tenancy and all your crofting rights will be safeguarded. Please come along to the meeting and help us claim what is ours - the title to our land."

Following the meeting on the 27th June, Allan MacRae wrote again to Simon Laird to inform him that the crofters had now set up the Trust. He asked Laird to reconsider his previous request for a meeting because the crofters were keen to discuss with him any possibility there might be for a re-arrangement of the lots to make the purchase of the croft lands a more practical proposition, given Laird's comment "... that the lots were arranged to allow the crofters to make a bid for the title to our land."[94] Allan MacRae repeated his request that any other offers for the estate would be made in the knowledge of the crofters' intentions to acquire the land under the right to buy provisions of the Crofting Acts if they failed in their bid. It was very important that the selling agents and the liquidator were left in no doubt as to the sincerity of the crofters and of their feelings.

The next few weeks were taken up with meetings with the various public bodies and other potential providers of funds and with the preparation of the feasibility study and business plan, first drafts of which were produced towards the end of July. The Trust issued a press release on 26th July to announce the public meeting of the crofters for the 28th July which launched the public appeal for funds. We have seen earlier in this Chapter how this meeting captured the imagination of the Press, but it is interesting to note that, at this stage, it had not finally been decided that the Trust should acquire the whole estate. Bill Ritchie outlined to the meeting the three options which were available. A bid for the whole estate, taking in partners if necessary (presumably a

reference to the possibility of a joint venture with
organisations such as the John Muir Trust or the RSPB);
a bid for the whole estate except the croft lands; and the
fall back option of acquiring the croft lands through the right
to buy provisions of the Crofting Acts.

Following the public meeting on the 28th July, Bill
Ritchie wrote to Simon Laird at the selling agents and told
him that the crofters were working hard to prepare a bid for
the first closing date. He ended by saying: "The Assynt case
is beginning to take on a larger dimension throughout the
Highlands and it would be good to achieve a sensible
outcome if at all possible."[95] On 24th August, John Clegg &
Co announced the closing date for offers for the estate to be
12 noon on 16th September and on the 27th August a
meeting was held between representatives of the Trust, the
selling agents, the liquidator (Raymond Hocking from the
City of London firm Stoy Hayward) and Savilles (who were
the estate factor). This was a defining moment in the bid
because it was at this meeting that the liquidator became
aware, possibly for the first time, of how well the crofters
were organised, of the strength of their purpose and of their
passion. Simon Fraser recalls that the liquidator was
impressed, in particular, by the dignity of the Trust's case.
Graeme Scott, who was also present at the meeting,
especially recalls the effect Allan MacRae had on the
liquidator and his advisers. While liquidators are well used,
in the course of their professional lives, to meetings with
disparate groups of people, there is little doubt that the
liquidator here could not have been expecting a man such
as MacRae. With perfect timing, Allan MacRae produced
what Scott describes as a show stopping statement. "My
people," declared MacRae, "have been on this land for
centuries. It is our land," he said, "and we mean to have our
land." His words and, more particularly, the passion so

clearly behind them and the manner of their delivery
stunned the meeting. If the liquidator had had any illusions
that the Assynt crofters could be disregarded, this meeting
and MacRae's intervention, destroyed them.

• The estate assets are considered •

Further discussions and preparation for the bid continued
during August and the business plan and feasibility study
were finalised. At the beginning of September, Simon Fraser
reported to the steering group on his examination of the title
to the estate. A number of interesting points arose. The sale
particulars in 1989 and, again in 1992 stated that the right
to minerals was excluded from the sale and so "... the
opportunities for a superquarry are absent from the
inventory."[96] In fact, Simon Fraser had discovered that the
minerals were included in the seller's title to the land and so
a bid for the land would include the mineral rights.
Secondly, the salmon fishing rights included in the sale were
clarified. These salmon fishings in the sea were from Rubha
Rodha on the south of Loch Roe to Rubha na Maoile on the
east of Loch Nedd, together with the store and ice house at
Culkein, Achnacarnin and the store at Clachtoll. While the
salmon fishing rights in the sea had been sold to SPS in 1989,
they had subsequently been transferred back to Assynt
Trading Company Limited (the Vestey estate company)
under the condition that Assynt Trading Company would
not exercise its right to use the fishings. Furthermore, that
transfer back to Assynt Trading Company had excluded the
right to net at Clachtoll and Culkein, but these rights had
been leased back to a Vestey company for a period of fifty
years. On the face of it this might have appeared an odd
situation, but of course the Assynt Estate to the south of the
North Lochinver Estate included the valuable migratory

rivers Inver and Kirkaig and the effective freeze put on
netting in the coastal waters to the north round to Loch Nedd
which these arrangements achieved, would protect the
Assynt Estate fishing in the Inver and the Kirkaig. But the
effect of the arrangements was also that the sea fishing rights
to salmon which were included in the title were, in effect,
limited to the right to net at Clachtoll and Culkein when the
fifty year lease expired. Lastly, the sale particulars had
referred to a right to put one boat on Loch Assynt to fish for
salmon, sea trout and char. In fact, the title included the right
for two boats with various other rights of access, mooring
facilities and the right to erect a boathouse.

Meetings of the steering group on the 2nd and 8th
September discussed the strategy for the bid and the group
was brought up to date with developments on the raising of
funds. By the 8th September, the amount raised by donations
and pledges had reached £95,000 and the Highland
Prospect loan and the CASE grant had been confirmed.
Discussions were still proceeding with SNH, and the
Highland Regional Council grant had not yet been
confirmed. However, the steering group felt confident
enough that the bid could, and indeed should, be for the
whole estate (excluding the decrofted cottage at Clashmore).
The actual level at which the bid should be submitted was,
of course, crucial. There was a strong feeling within the
steering group that the bid should not be allowed to fail
because it was pitched too low; if this should happen it was
believed that all those who had given donations and made
pledges would feel let down. Having regard to the monies
available and likely, at that stage, to become available, it was
thought, on 2nd September, that a bid of £235,000 was
appropriate, although this was increased to £245,000 at the
meeting on the 8th September. We saw, earlier in this
Chapter, the issues which confronted the steering group in

relation to Torbreck Lodge and the £90,000 loan from Highland Prospect. In many ways it was a bold decision to include Torbreck Lodge in the bid and Bill Ritchie has described it as being 'really nerve wracking'. At that stage there was no firm view as to whether Torbreck Lodge should be sold as soon as possible after the purchase to repay the Highland Prospect loan before the rate of interest on the loan changed to a commercial rate, or whether it should be kept to generate an income for the Trust from renting out fishing and shooting rights. Certainly the rental would cover the interest payable for the initial period of the loan, but Bill Ritchie thought that the long term objective would be for the Trust to sell Torbreck Lodge.

• The first bid is made - and rejected •

And so, on the 9th September, 1992 Simon Fraser's firm, Anderson, Macarthur & Co, wrote to John Clegg & Co on behalf of the Trust with the formal offer of £235,000 for the whole estate apart from lot 3, being the cottage at 208 Clashmore. The offer was expressed to be open for acceptance by 12 noon on 23rd September. There then followed an anxious period of waiting. On the closing date of 16th September the selling agents issued a press release stating that they "... were pleased with the choice of offers received, which included suggestions for the whole estate, combinations of Lots and individual Lots. The Liquidator is seeking clarification on certain facts and conditions which will enable him to make a further announcement at 4 p.m on Friday 18th September. We should emphasise that all offers received are being carefully considered." This delay was clearly disappointing to the crofters and raised the level of anxiety, particularly as the press release had suggested that offers apart from the Trust's had also been received; it was reported in *The Independent* that the selling agents had claimed to have received eleven offers.[97] As Bill Ritchie said: "These have been tense moments. It is deflating, but all we can do is wait and see. We are confident of the justice of our case, and that we have made a sensible offer based on valuations."[98] John MacKenzie was, at least on the surface, more phlegmatic: "I have a slight sense of anti-climax but I have now returned to the relaxed attitude I have adopted throughout the entire episode. We are still determined that the entire assets of the North Lochinver Estate is our objective."[99] In fact, it was not until the 22nd September that the selling agents announced that the Trust's bid, along with all the others, had been rejected. The press release issued by John Clegg & Co was short and to the point: "Following the closing date last week (16th September, 1992) the liquidator has considered carefully the various proposals submitted and at this stage has indicated that none of the offers received are acceptable." This was a blow to the crofters although the main concern, that there would be another major purchaser, appeared to have dissipated. However, the crofters began to feel that there was an element of discrimination involved in the rejection of their bid. Allan MacRae said: "I think crofters will feel bitterly disappointed and suspect what the motives are in refusing our offer."[100] and: "Something inside me tells me they don't want us to have the land. That's my gut reaction."[101] Statements by Crowe, John Clegg & Co's senior partner, suggesting that the liquidator was considering running the estate for a period in the hope that conditions for land sales might improve were clearly not helpful: "The view [as to rejection of the offers] might change tomorrow, next week, next month or they might keep it for five years, I just don't know."[102] In fact the suggestion that the liquidator might run the estate for a period was not one which, on the face of it, appeared to be consistent with liquidation law and indeed John MacKenzie was quick to point this out: "We are not trained in law but it appears to us that the liquidator is beginning to act as a receiver when there is talk of running the estate for five years."[103] But the statement was nonetheless disturbing. The crofters were keen that the situation should be resolved as soon as possible and they knew that delay would not operate in their favour. A further statement by Crowe also upset the crofters. This was his invitation for bidders to negotiate privately with the selling agents: "If any of the existing batch of offerors wish to improve their offers, or come back with alternative suggestions or whatever, we are in the business of listening to those suggestions and we'll just take it forward stage by stage."[104] John MacKenzie commented: "... I personally would question the ethics of the way they have handled this, almost keeping our offer on the back burner while they look to negotiate with others."[105]

• The second bid is made - and rejected •

This war of words notwithstanding, the Trust immediately put in a revised offer of £245,000, open for acceptance until 29th September. The letter from Anderson, Macarthur & Co accompanying the revised offer made the point that while the aspirations of the liquidator and of the principal creditors of SPS may not be met by this sum, it should be borne in mind that the vast proportion of the land was subject to crofting tenure. Disregarding the sporting and mineral rights, the land could not have a value much in excess of its crofting value - fifteen times the croft rentals - approximately £40,000. The letter spelled out very clearly the fallback solution if the revised offer was not accepted. It was "... the intention of all of the crofters on the estate to purchase all of the croft land under the provisions of the Crofting Reform

(Scotland) Act 1976. First, the inbye land of all the crofts will be purchased, then the common grazings will be apportioned and purchased. Your clients will not realise more than £40,000 - before expenses. While this process may take some considerable time and will occasion considerable expense to both parties, our clients are quite determined to see the process through to the end and the events of last week [a reference to the comments of John Clegg & Co referred to above] have if anything greatly strengthened their determination. We cannot imagine that any other party would be particularly interested in acquiring the land while this process was going ahead."

This revised offer was accompanied by a press release issued by the Trust which reflected the concerns of the crofters at the turn of events. It stressed that the offer was made in good faith and that the crofters were to "... seek an assurance from the liquidator that the main creditor, believed to be a foreign bank, is fully aware that what is for sale is not a sporting estate or a wild life paradise but 99% croft land occupied by crofters and regulated by the Crofting Acts. The crofters are to question the statement made by Angus Crow of Clegg & Co the selling agent, to the press that the liquidator would continue to run the estate for months even 'five years' rather than accept the crofters' offer based on these independent valuations. The crofters' offer is widely believed to be the best received. Crofters ... also question the ethics of the selling agent and liquidator of inviting the Assynt Crofters to make a sealed offer and then literally minutes after rejecting the offer publicly inviting anyone to negotiate privately with the liquidator in the knowledge of the crofters' offer. The crofters are to seek legal advice on this matter."[106]

The second bid by the Trust was rejected at the end of September and on being informed of this decision, Bill

Ritchie said: "We have been informed that our offer in its present form is unacceptable. Messrs John Clegg & Co, estate agents, are to be instructed by the liquidator to enter into negotiations with the crofters to see whether a revised offer can be put forward for consideration. Crofters' representatives are now taking legal advice and will make proposals in a meeting in Stoer tonight."[107] John MacKenzie was more blunt: "We have made clear that this was our final offer. So far as I can see we will be moving to the next stage of our strategy and using the terms of the 1976 Act to buy the title to our crofts."[108]   Another crofter was blunter still: "It looks like war."[109]

• If we have to take it piece by piece through the Land Court, so be it. But take it we will •

At the public meeting of the crofters on the 1st October, Bill Ritchie told the disappointed crofters that all was not lost; indeed he was quite positive, saying that the crofters had achieved everything they had, in fact, set out to achieve. They had, so far, stopped the break-up of the estate, they had, so far, stopped the sale and, so far as could be judged, they had put everyone else out of the market. He made it clear that in any subsequent negotiations with the selling agents the crofters would not sacrifice their principles just to get the lands: "It is not incumbent upon us to start squandering our money and other people's money, our families' money in this market. That is not what we set out to do ... We are making a genuine offer based on valuations. We cannot be dragged into a spiralling competition." He then told the meeting that the fallback solution of using the right to buy provisions of the Crofting Acts would be used. Allan MacRae ended the meeting and the crofters left with his words ringing in their ears: "There is no doubt of our determination to acquire the land, one way or another. If we have to take it piece by piece through the Land Court, so be it. But take it we will."[110]

The second offer from the Trust was left open and the parties retired to reconsider their respective positions. The Trust had always had a concern that the principal creditor of SPS, believed to be a foreign bank, might not be fully aware of the realities of the situation and of the almost wholly crofting tenure of the estate and the implications this had as to value. The Trust established, shortly after the second bid was rejected, that the principal creditor was, in fact, Ostgota Enskilda Bank of Stockholm, and determined to write to the Bank to make them fully aware of the situation. Bill Ritchie wrote to the Bank on 7th October in colourful terms. He explained the background to the offer and stressed that the North Lochinver Estate was not a valuable sporting estate, but a crofting one: "If you believe that you were at all misled as to the true value of our croft lands and led to believe that it was a sporting estate, we want to assure you that we have protested to the selling agents and to others that this is not the case. The North Lochinver Estate consists almost entirely of croft lands regulated by the Crofting Acts of Scotland." The letter went on in increasingly passionate terms: "We have no wish to exercise our legal rights as tenants to buy the title to our lands against innocent parties. But as our patience and the patience of the whole Scottish people including the 12,000 crofters is at an end, we can no longer stand by and watch our land being traded as paper assets and people like yourselves, who may be innocent of the legal status of these lands, perhaps being misled with possible serious conse-quences. Not only for the purchaser but also for the crofter tenants." The letter offered an explanation of the rights of the crofters under the Crofting Acts and offered a meeting between representatives of the Trust and the Bank as a way forward to resolve the matter. Warming to his task, Bill Ritchie continued his letter with a somewhat exaggerated description of the support the crofters had and ended with something of a tirade against the evils of landownership in the Highlands: "With the support of virtually the whole of the Scottish nation (you will be aware of the interest of the Press, Radio and Television in this case) the Government agencies and all political parties including Government ministers, the Assynt Crofters want to purchase the whole of the estate to demonstrate that we can protect our economic, cultural and natural heritage and our future for our families. And protect it against the speculators and dealers who would use our lands as assets for other ventures. We would stress that we do not believe that you are deliberately standing in the way of our just ambition to save our land but rather that you are not fully aware of the implications of this case that you are caught up in, and indeed may not be aware of the outrage of the Scottish people at the way we have been treated over this attempt to break up and sell our croft lands."[111] It is interesting to speculate on the effects this letter may have had on a group of Swedish bankers. It is reasonably certain that, if nothing else, they will have wished that their security was over land which was not in one of the seven crofting counties, and if they were encouraged by the letter to become better acquainted with the intricacies of crofting law, the experience will have done nothing to change that wish. In fact their response to that letter was a deafening silence and it was only when Bill Ritchie sent a fax on the 27th October asking for the Bank's confirmation that they had received the letter that the Bank responded with a one line fax by return confirming that the Bank had, indeed, received the letter. The Bank may well have felt under further pressure when Comann Ceilteach Oilthigh Obar-Dheadhain (the Celtic Society of Aberdeen University) wrote to various trade unions in Sweden urging the unions to take up the cause of the Assynt crofters. The letter asked: "... the Swedish people for their help to put pressure on the Ostgota Bank to respect the lives of hundreds of Scots. These people have been on that land for hundreds of years and deserve consideration from a Swedish corporation that would not allow the same to happen in Sweden." One newspaper offered to fly Allan MacRae to Sweden to meet with the Bank. In the event, however, the Bank was not willing to meet with representatives of the steering group.

• The Manse Loch strategy •

At the public meeting of the crofters at the end of September, the steering group had warned that the fallback option could well now be activated. During October, discussions were held as to how to put this plan into action. The right to buy provisions apply to the croft house, the croft land and the common grazings, but only to the extent that the common grazings have been apportioned to the croft, and then only if those common grazings are contiguous with the croft - in other words in actual contact with or touching the croft land - or are adjacent - close to or neighbouring the croft land.[112] The usual conditions which would apply to the granting of an apportionment would include the erection of a stockproof fence. Application would have to be made to the Crofters Commission and the landlord would be entitled to raise objections. There would clearly be a considerable amount of work to be done, and considerable cooperation from all the crofters, if application was to be made for the common grazings on the whole estate to be apportioned and for each croft to be purchased. The steering group therefore decided to target an initial area where it was believed that exercise of the right to buy provisions would most effectively devalue the estate in the hands of the liquidator. A meeting was held between the crofters in the Achmelvich and Torbreck townships to discuss what became known as the Manse Loch strategy. It will be recalled that not all the crofts in the Achmelvich township were, in fact, included in the estate, although all the common grazings were. At first sight, therefore, it might appear that Achmelvich was not the most appropriate township to choose. But Bill Ritchie had crofts in the township and Allan MacRae was in the neighbouring township of Torbreck and so key personalities would be involved. But more importantly, and as we have seen earlier in this Chapter, it was thought that the Manse Loch system when linked to Torbreck House was the most valuable asset in the estate so far as the liquidator was concerned. The Manse Loch, the river running from that loch to Loch Fasg an t-Seana Chlaidh, that loch, Loch an Saile and the river running from Loch an Saile into Loch Roe had been described in the sale particulars as providing '... a superb opportunity to develop an interesting and rewarding fishery in a beautiful unspoilt situation.' While '... recent catches have been modest, reflecting the token effort that has been put into the fishing of this river over the past few years ...' it was said that '... in years gone by the river system produced exciting sea trout and salmon fishing and there seems little reason why rewarding improvements could not be made to recreate this asset.'

The river system marked the boundary between the Achmelvich and Torbreck townships and so joint action by the two townships would be required. As is explained in the Appendix, when the right to buy provisions of the Crofting Acts are exercised, the crofter does not acquire the salmon fishing rights. However, the landlord is not able to retain the exclusive right to fish for trout and so acquisition of the croft lands and common grazings adjoining the river system

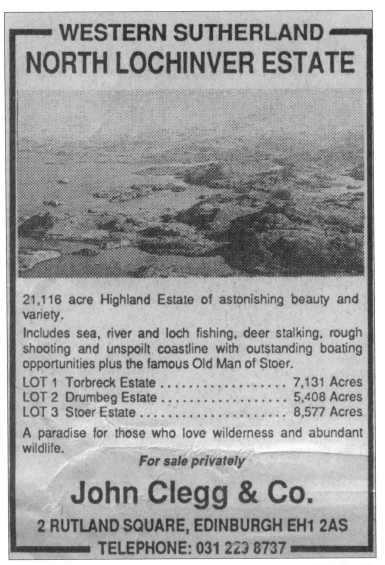

WESTERN SUTHERLAND
NORTH LOCHINVER ESTATE

21,116 acre Highland Estate of astonishing beauty and variety.

Includes sea, river and loch fishing, deer stalking, rough shooting and unspoilt coastline with outstanding boating opportunities plus the famous Old Man of Stoer.

LOT 1 Torbreck Estate . . . . 7,131 Acres
LOT 2 Drumbeg Estate . . . . 5,408 Acres
LOT 3 Stoer Estate . . . . 8,577 Acres

A paradise for those who love wilderness and abundant wildlife.

For sale privately

John Clegg & Co.

2 RUTLAND SQUARE, EDINBURGH EH1 2AS
TELEPHONE: 031 229 8737

The Estate is offered for sale in 1989.

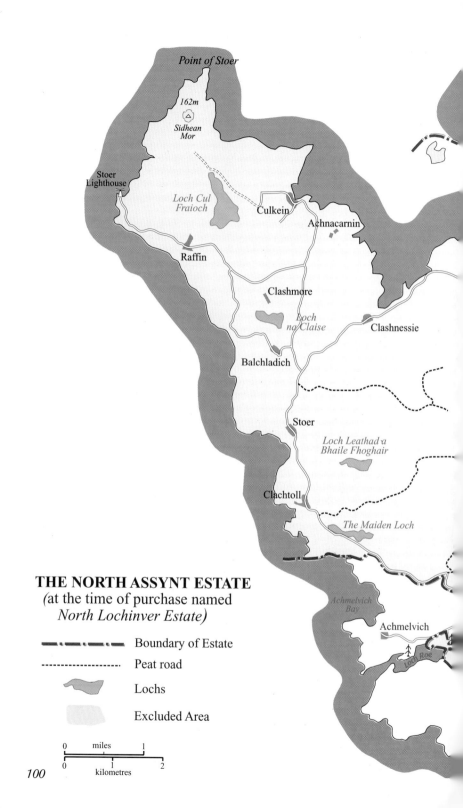

Point of Stoer

162m
Sidhean Mor

Stoer Lighthouse

Loch Cul Fraioch

Culkein

Achnacarnin

Raffin

Clashmore

Loch na Claise

Clashnessie

Balchladich

Stoer

Loch Leathad a Bhaile Fhoghair

Clachtoll

The Maiden Loch

THE NORTH ASSYNT ESTATE
*(*at the time of purchase named
North Lochinver Estate)

Boundary of Estate

Peat road

Lochs

Excluded Area

Achmelvich Bay

Achmelvich

Loch Roe

0   miles   1

0   1   2
kilometres

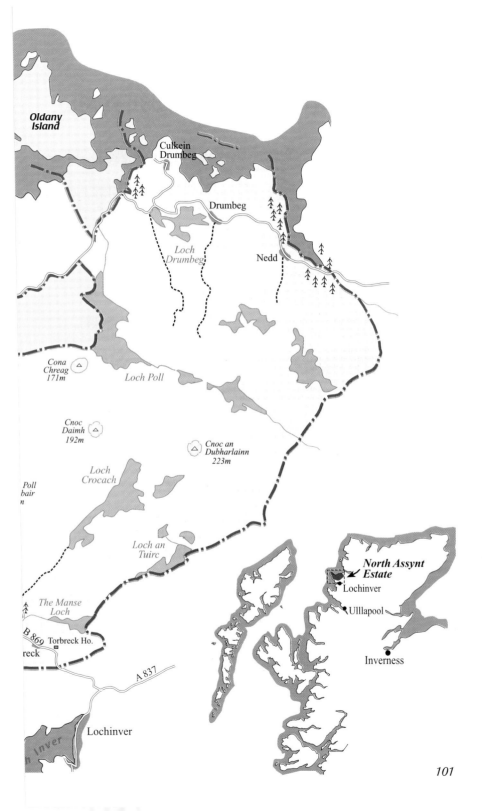

Oldany
Island

Culkein
Drumbeg

Drumbeg

Loch
Drumbeg

Nedd

Cona
Chreag
171m

Loch Poll

Cnoc
Daimh
192m

Cnoc an
Dubharlainn
223m

Loch
Crocach

Poll
bair
n

Loch an
Tuirc

The Manse
Loch

B 869
Torbreck Ho.

reck

A 837

Lochinver

North Assynt
Estate

Lochinver

Ulllapool

Inverness

28/7/92.   Assynt Crofters Trust

Public meeting at Stoer primary school
    Launch of Assynt Crofters Trust Appeal

Alan opened the meeting and thanked the large number of
people (approx 120) for attending, in particular, M.P. Mr Robert
McLennan. Also present were T.V. cameras and reporters.
Alan then thanked Bill who he said was very much the
architect of the plan to buy the estate
    Bill thanked all present for the support given He said the
plan was to safeguard the land and the future by offering a
fair price for the estate. We had a just claim, and would
make a just offer. If we failed we would then go to the
land court and demand title to our land.
    Tremendous support had already been given by various
groups. Andrew Thin of C.A.S.E. had granted money for a
business plan
    It was hoped to achieve charitable status, but this was
not easy, though it would be very helpful in raising funds
    If our appeal should be successful it should be possible
to make affordable housing available for young local people
Perhaps even in time to create local jobs
    It was hoped that money could be raised before the deadline
Three options were available
    1.) offer bid for everything, taking a partner if necessary
    2.) offer bid for everything except non-croft land
    3.) acquire title though fall back position ie land court
Whatever would happen, we were optimistic for the future.
Alan then introduced Robert McLennan who gave a
very emotional speech about his forbears originally being
cleared from the Ullapool area, and how he could identify
without cause. He then pledged fifty pounds for each of his
twenty six years in Parliament. This was met by thunderous
applause. Forms were handed round, people were thanked for
coming, and the meeting closed about 9.30pm

Minutes of the meeting which launched the Public Appeal.

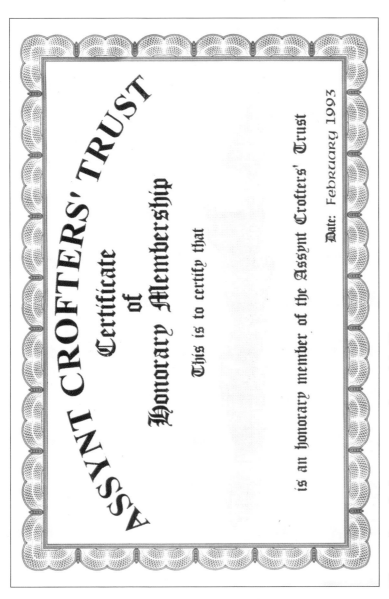

ASSYNT CROFTERS' TRUST

Certificate
of
Honorary Membership

This is to certify that

is an honorary member of the Assynt Crofters' Trust

Date: February 1993

The certificate for honorary members of the Trust.

Clashnessie Bay.

© *John MacPherson.*

(l-r) Duncan Kerr and Norman MacLeod and eleven members of the Steering Group - Allan MacRae, Alastair MacIntyre, Felicite Basu, Donald MacKenzie, Hughie Matheson, John MacKenzie, Bill Ritchie, Derek MacLeod, Aileen Kinnaird, Ishbel MacAuley, Pat MacPhail.

© *Am Bratach (Donald MacLeod).*

John MacKenzie and Ben at Culkein Drumbeg.

A potential purchaser is rescued by the crofters
from Clashnessie beach.

Simon Fraser in conversation with Bill Ritchie.

*John MacKenzie, Allan Macrae and Bill Ritchie
tell the crofters the second bid has been rejected.*

Loch Drumbeg and Quinag.

© John MacPherson.

111

Croft at Balchladich Bay.

© John MacPherson.

Loch na Claise.

113

Crofts at Achnacarnin/Culkein.

Common grazings at Stoer.

© *John MacPherson.*

Looking south east from the Point of Stoer.

117

Stoer Lighthouse.

119

The split rock at Clachtoll.

John MacKenzie, Bill Ritchie and Allan MacRae at Clachtoll.

Clashmore.

Canisp, Suilven and the road south from Clachtoll.

ASSYNT CROFTERS TRUST

tel 05714 315 fax 05714 558

Lochinver
Assynt
Sutherland
IV27 4JB

1st February 1993

Dear Friend

Today, with your help, we have created history as we take over our croft land and embark on the great challenge of managing our resources free from the burden of absentee landlords.

Your support has been vital to our success and the Assynt Crofters will never forget that. We are creating a Register of Support to be placed in Stoer Post Office to let everyone know who supported us.

All of the crofters thank you for your support and hope that the changes you helped to create will lead the way in crofting throughout the Highlands and Islands.

Thank you.

The Trust takes possession of the Estate.

Bill Ritchie celebrates the Trust's success 8th December, 1992.

Assynt Crofters Trust

CELEBRATION CEILIDH/DANCE

at CULAG HOTEL, LOCHINVER

on FRIDAY, 5th FEBRUARY, 1993

at 8 p.m.

Tickets £5.00

An invitation to the celebration cèilidh.

would allow the crofters access to the trout fishing and to allow the Trust to grant fishing permits on the river. Furthermore, the Trust would be entitled to an indemnity from the liquidator (as the estate owner) for any loss or damage arising from the exercise by the landlord of his right of access for fishing; this would all undoubtedly have some devaluing effect on the estate in the hands of the liquidator.

The strategy would have a further desirable effect so far as the crofters were concerned. Deer are a constant problem to crofters due to the damage they cause to crops, pasture and trees. This is particularly so when crofts are in close proximity to a sporting estate. Deer are a game reserved to the landlord under the Crofting Acts although the crofter is entitled to damages for damage caused by deer. When the crofter exercises his right to buy under the Crofting Acts, the landlord is, as we see in the Appendix, entitled to retain the shooting rights through a sporting lease. However, the crofter is given limited rights to kill deer which are causing damage. First, if the Red Deer Commission is satisfied that red deer are causing serious damage to forestry, or to agricultural production, on any agricultural ground, woodland or garden ground or are causing injury to farm animals (for example by overgrazing of pasture), and considers that killing the deer is necessary to prevent further damage or injury, then the Commission will authorise the killing of the deer; these are the so called 'marauding deer' provisions.[113] In addition, the occupier of land has the right to kill deer on arable land, garden ground and land laid down in permanent grass, if the deer are causing serious damage;[114] this right does not, however, apply to moorland or unenclosed land and so the right would not normally exist on common grazings. However, the fencing required to effect the apportionment of the common grazings on the Achmelvich and Torbreck townships and the reseeding of these grazings would change the status of the lands to permanent grass, and deer straying on these lands could be killed. Again, this would have a devaluing effect on the estate lands left in the hands of the liquidator.

Articles in *The Herald*:[115] Crofters Refine Tactics in Battle of Assynt, in the *Press & Journal*:[116] Assynt Crofters Change Tactics - Trust Set to Target Migratory Fishings in Land Court Move, and in *The Northern Times*[117] reported this development and *The Herald* article disclosed that '... the crofters have recently flown in by helicopter more than six tonnes of fencing materials and have nearly completed 3km of fencing around the best grazing in the area.'

• Attitudes harden •

That attitudes might be said to have been hardening in this period and that historical anti-landlord feelings were being kept in check with difficulty, is evidenced by two other matters which were covered in the press, and while they had no direct bearing on the purchase of the North Lochinver Estate, they are revealing of the crofter antipathy towards landlords, and the depths of emotions in relation to landlords felt by crofters, and help to explain the intense desire of the crofters in the area to have control of their own assets and affairs.

On 24th October, *The Scotsman* had published an article by Ruth Wishart under the headline: 'United They Stand'. In the article, and referring to the time when the North Lochinver Estate formed part of Edmund Vestey's Assynt Estate, she said: "Over the years of private ownership they [the crofters] have indeed felt an alien element whose usefulness to their landlord, they suggest, was calculated solely in their ability to maximise his profits. They claim he thwarted any local initiative which might challenge the

monopoly status enjoyed by his local commercial outlets."
Mr Vestey took issue with this and, in a letter to *The
Scotsman*[118] sought to correct some misleading impressions he
believed may have arisen from the article - in particular in
relation to the harbour development and land for houses in
Inver Park in Lochinver. He ended his letter by saying: "I
have known and loved Lochinver since I was three. My first
schooling was there and I have always done my best to
encourage sensible development where it will not spoil the
whole character, which makes it the marvellous place it is."
A response to this letter from Bill Ritchie and John
MacKenzie was not, however, published by *The Scotsman*. A
subsequent article by Judith Napier in the *Press & Journal*
reported that: "Lochinver residents and their local councillor
have reacted with astonishment to claims by landowner
Edmund Vestey that he has always encouraged development
in the area." The article included the trenchant views of
Councillor Keith Francis on the alleged role of Edmund
Vestey in the development of Lochinver.[119]

The other issue reported concerned an elderly lady, Miss
Nan Macleod who had, in fact, died in 1991. Miss Macleod
had occupied a cottar house in Stoer until her death and had
sought to have her house improved with the aid of grant.
Under the Crofting Acts a cottar has the right to buy the
house,[120] but Miss Macleod had signed a lease of the house
from the estate which, of course, meant that she could not
bequeath the house in her will, as she could have done if she
had exercised her right to buy. Following her death, it was
reported that Savilles, the land agents who were administer-
ing the North Lochinver Estate on behalf of SPS, had
threatened court action to gain possession of the house.
Concern was expressed over a number of alleged similar
incidents and the actions of Savilles were described as being
'insensitive and illtimed'. John MacKenzie said that he knew

that many people were surprised by the determination of the crofters to control their own land but that perhaps these events gave an example of the reason for this. He was particularly concerned, given that a relative of his had suffered in similar circumstances and he was aware of ten other, similar, cases. He went on to say that when (not if) the Trust acquired the North Lochinver Estate the leases of any other tenant in a similar situation would be revoked to give them absolute rights of inheritance. Again, there was press coverage of this story. *The Northern Times*.[121] Assynt Crofters Have Suspicions Over House Leases, the *Press & Journal*.[122] Assynt Crofters Hit at Agents over Leases, and in the November edition of *Am Bratach*.

• But discussions continue •

However, while a certain amount of public posturing might have been taking place, behind the scenes discussions were still proceeding between the Trust and the selling agents, and Simon Fraser met with the selling agents towards the end of October. He explained that, while he was not in a position to negotiate, if the selling agents had any firm proposals to make, they ought to do so. He also explained to the selling agents that the Trust was determined to keep to certain principles - that all of the crofting lands should be acquired and that the maximum possible of other available resources should be acquired so that they could be used for the best possible good of the community, and that if the Trust was to acquire less than the whole estate, then the price would be reduced accordingly. The selling agents apparently took the view that it was extremely unlikely that the level of the Trust's offer of £245,000 could be raised and so they wrote to the Trust with proposals that the Trust should submit a revised offer, but on the basis that certain assets should be excluded from the sale. These assets were: Torbreck House, the right to put two boats on Loch Assynt, Lot 4, the right to shoot three stags per year on the estate and the Manse Loch river system and the right to put boats on the lochs in the system, Loch Dubh at Ardroe, Loch Crocach and Loch Preas nan Aighean. It was clear that the strategy behind this was for the selling agents to realise a larger sum of money for the excluded assets than the amount by which the Trust would reduce its bid. This alternative proposal was considered by the steering group. Any move to acquire less than the whole estate would mean going back to the public bodies who had provided funds on the whole estate basis. Furthermore, there was a feeling that, given the success of the public fund raising campaign, the Trust was now morally bound to acquire the whole estate. So this approach was rejected by the Trust. Bill Ritchie wrote, on 16th November, to the people who had given pledges of money to the Trust. He said that he had hoped to have been able to write before to let them know of the Trust's success. "But things are dragging on longer than we thought." However he remained optimistic: "Be assured that we have not weakened in our resolve. With your continued support we will win this historical battle for the right to our land and its resources. We have a fair offer on the table and history and justice on our side."[123] Enclosed with each letter was a car sticker which said: "I support the Assynt Crofters". The car stickers were not just seen locally. John MacKenzie received a letter from a Mr MacMillan who had sent a donation from New Zealand and in which he described how he had driven into a supermarket car park there to find that the car next to his also had the sticker proudly displayed in the rear window!

• It looks like we have a deal •

There then followed a critical period, and one which was marked, for the first time, by the Trust aiming to keep a low profile in terms of publicity and speculation. Simon Fraser had a meeting on 23rd November with the selling agents, the liquidator and representatives of Ostgota Enskilda Bank. Fraser came away from that meeting with the impression that the liquidator was close to making a decision to sell the estate to the Trust, but that the Trust would have to make a significant increase in its offer of £245,000. The liquidator clearly had a difficult pill to swallow in terms of an estate now valued at a price in the region of £400,000 but with (probably) the highest offer standing at less than £250,000, when it had been purchased only three years earlier for a sum in excess of £1,000,000. Simon Fraser was also concerned that there was still the possibility of another bid coming in for the non croft assets - Torbreck House, the Manse Loch fishing system (notwithstanding the Trust's 'Manse Loch strategy' explained above), and so on. If this happened and it succeeded there is little doubt that the whole rationale of the Trust and what it was trying to achieve would have collapsed. Simon Fraser reported on his meeting to the steering group and it was decided that he should be given full negotiating authority to use all the monies available to the Trust. As at 25th November, the amount of donations received was £56,000 and the amount of pledges made was £74,000. The Trust clearly required some assurance that, if all the pledges could not be collected, the funds to cover the shortfall would be available. The Highland Fund came forward with an agreement to underwrite any such shortfall. This support was not, in fact, widely reported although the January edition of *Am Bratach* revealed this crucial role performed by the Highland Fund.

And so on 27th November Simon Fraser submitted, on behalf of the Trust, a revised offer of £265,000 recognising that the Trust could, and probably would have to, go higher. In the event, the Trust did have to go higher and, on the 4th December, Simon Fraser submitted a bid of £300,000 making it quite clear that this was, indeed, the Trust's final offer.

After a tense wait of four days, the success of the Assynt Crofters' Trust bid was announced by a brief telephone call from Simon Laird to Simon Fraser. With the words "it looks like we have a deal," Laird announced the success of the Trust. Celebrations followed, and on Monday 1st February 1993, the Assynt Crofters' Trust became the legal owner of the North Lochinver Estate.

Notes

1   In the case of Achmelvich, the Estate only includes some of the crofts, the remaining ones still being within the Assynt Estate. However, all the common grazings are within the North Lochinver Estate.

2   MacPhail, Isobel, Sustaining Life and Land, in Mollison, Denis (ed), *Sharing the Land,* John Muir Trust, 1994, p. 52

3   Bangor-Jones, Malcolm, The Establishment of Crofting in North West Sutherland, *Am Bratach,* June and July, 1993

4   See, e.g. Hunter, James, *The Creation of the Crofting Community*, Edinburgh, 1976 and Devine,T. M., *Clanship to Crofters' War-The social transformation of the Scottish Highlands*, Manchester and New York, 1994. For the clearances in Assynt, see Bangor-Jones, Malcolm, *The Assynt Clearances*, Dundee 1998

5   Adam, R. J., *Papers on Sutherland Estate Management*, Edinburgh, 1972, vol 1, p. 127

6   *Napier Report*, Q27044

7   In fact it appears that this evidence is misleading, Ardvar having been cleared well before the 1830s - see Bangor-Jones, Malcolm, *The Clearances in Assynt*, Dundee, 1998, p. 47

8   *Napier Report*, Q27218, 27219 and 27221

9   *Napier Report*, Q27232

10 *Napier Report*, Q27658

11 *Napier Report*, Q27687 and 27688

12 Bangor-Jones, Malcolm, Assynt Resists, *Am Bratach,* Jan-March, 1995, Macphail, I. M. M., *The Crofters' War,* Stornoway, 1989, pp. 144 and 145 and MacKenzie, John, *Land Tenure in Assynt and the Formation of the Assynt Crofters' Trust,* Comunn Eachdraidh Asainte, Stoer, 1997

13 Hugh Kerr's great great granddaughter, Dolina Kerr, lives today in Clashmore

14 MacKenzie, John, *Land Tenure in Assynt and the Formation of the Assynt Crofters' Trust* , Comunn Eachdraidh Asainte, Stoer, 1997

15 Quoted in Cramb, Auslan, *Who Owns Scotland Now? The use and abuse of private land,* Edinburgh and London, 1996, p. 41

16 MacKenzie, John, *Land Tenure in Assynt and the formation of the Assynt Crofters' Trust,* Comunn Eachdraidh Asainte, Stoer, 1997

17 MacKenzie, John, *Land Tenure in Assynt and the formation of the Assynt Crofters' Trust,* Comunn Eachdraidh Asainte, Stoer, 1997

18 See the Appendix

19 BBC Landward, 6th September, 1992

20 7th August, 1992

21 See further in Chapter 5

22 Meek, Donald E., The Role of Song in the Highland Land Agitation, *Scottish Gaelic Studies,* vol 16, 1990, p. 8

23 Meek, Donald E., *Tuath Is Tighearna - Tenants and Landlords,* Edinburgh, 1995, pp. 201 & 202

24 Thomson, Derick, *An Introduction to Gaelic Poetry,* Edinburgh, 1974 and 1990, p. 236

25 Meek, Donald E., The Role of Song in the Highland Land Agitation, *Scottish Gaelic Studies,* vol 16, 1990, p. 8

26 Hunter, James, *On the Other Side of Sorrow,* Edinburgh, 1995

27 BBC Landward , 6th September 1992. But there are others who do not take the same view. Speaking in the Grampian Television programme

broadcast on 13th December 1993, Neil Graham-Campbell of the land
agents Finlayson-Hughes said: "... the best conservationist is the good old
fashioned Victorian landlord who keeps all the people away. The worst
thing for conservation is the disturbance of human beings."

28   SCU/ RSPB, Crofting and the Environment: A New Approach,
     Broadford and Edinburgh, 1992, quoted in Hunter, James, *On the Other
     Side of Sorrow*, Edinburgh, 1995, p. 165
29   *The Herald,* 11th June, 1992
30   *Press and Journal,* 11th June, 1992
31   *The Scotsman,* 12th June, 1992
32   *Whitbread v. Macdonald* [1992] SC, p. 479
33   *Whitbread v. Macdonald* [1992] SC, p. 485
34   BBC Landward, 6th September, 1992, and quoted in Scenes, 1992,
     Scottish Environmental News in August, 1992, p. 3
35   Speaking in *BBC Landward,* transmitted on 6th September, 1992
36   See the Appendix
37   Of course, this would also be the case even where the Trust acquires the
     landlord's title.
38   *Consultation Paper on Possible Disposal of The Secretary of State for Scotland's
     Crofting Estates to Community Ownership,* Department of Agriculture and
     Fisheries for Scotland, February, 1990 (hereafter *The Consultation Paper,*
     February, 1990) and see also Chapter 5 below
39   Wightman, Andy, *Who Owns Scotland?* Edinburgh, p. 181. It should also
     be noted that the Company structure also has its difficulties. Under
     Company law the Directors of a Company owe their duties to the
     Company and occasions could arise when the Company's interest might
     conceivably diverge from that of the community which established it.
40   *Assynt Crofters' Trust Papers*
41   *SSC Evidence,* paras 76-77
42   *Am Bratach,* August, 1992
43   *Assynt Crofters' Trust Papers*
44   *Assynt Crofters' Trust Papers*
45   *Am Bratach,* November, 1992. In fact, David Laird, the Assynt Estate
     lawyer was related to Simon Laird
46   *The Scotsman*
47   Cramb, Auslan, *Who Owns Scotland Now? The use and abuse of private land,*
     Edinburgh and London, 1996, p.44
48   BBC Landward, 6th September, 1992
49   *Assynt Crofters' Trust Papers*
50   Quoted in *The Northern Times,* 31st July, 1992
51   Quoted in *The Northern Times,* 31st July, 1992
52   There were 81 such honorary members
53   The *West Highland Free Press,* 31st July, 1992
54   *The Northern Times,* 31st July, 1992
55   *The Guardian,* 31st July, 1992
56   *The Scotsman,* 29th July, 1992
57   *Press & Journal,* 29th July, 1992
58   *The Herald,* 29th July, 1992
59   *The Morning Star,* 29th July, 1992
60   Devine, T. M., *Clanship to Crofters' War-The social transformation of the
     Scottish Highlands,* Manchester and New York, 1994, p. 155
61   SCU/RSPB, *Crofting and the Environment: A New Approach,* Broadford and
     Edinburgh, 1992

62 *Assynt Crofters' Trust Papers*

63 Peter Peacock quoted in *The Herald,* 11th June, 1992

64 Quoted in *Am Bratach,* September 1992. John MacKenzie, however, recalls that Iain Robertson was initially opposed to the Trust and believes that it was the public support given by Sir Hector Munro, the then Minister of State at the Scottish Office, that caused the change of mind

65 *The Independent,* September, 1992

66 While the Ordnance Survey map names the loch as the Manse Loch (a reference to the old manse which overlooked the loch and which is now Torbreck Lodge) the old name for the loch as shown on the croft maps prepared in 1887, was Loch an Aite Mhòir. For a discussion on the importance of placenames in the Gaelic community and the dislocation felt by changes of names such as this, see Jedrej, C., and Nuttall, M., *White Settlers - The impact of rural repopulation in Scotland,* Luxembourg, 1996, pp. 123-127

67 Letter of 11th July, 1992, *Assynt Crofters' Trust Papers*

68 Letter of 13th July, 1992, *Assynt Crofters' Trust Papers*

69 BBC Landward, 6th September, 1992

70 Made under section 9 of the Natural Heritage (Scotland) Act, 1991

71 See, e.g. Wightman, Andy, *Who Owns Scotland?* Edinburgh, pp. 182 to 186 and Wightman, Andy, A Perspective on Land Ownership, *Am Bratach,* nos 51 and 52, 1996

72 Quoted in *The Inverness Courier,* 15th September, 1992

73 Quoted in *The Herald,* 4th September, 1992

74 Quoted in the *Press & Journal,* 4th September, 1992. (Ironically, of course, the presence of blackthroated divers at Loch Poll would prove to be a problem - see p. 148)

75 *The Northern Times,* 11th September, 1992

76 *The Northern Times,* 11th September, 1992

77 *The Northern Times,* 11th September, 1992

78 See, for example, SCU/RSPB, *Crofting and the Environment: A New Approach,* Broadford and Edinburgh, 1992

79 Lister-Kaye, John, Ill Fares The Land, *Scottish Natural Heritage,* 1994, p. 14

80 Orr, Willie, *Deer Forests Landlords and Crofters,* Edinburgh, 1982, p. 148 and Hunter, James, *On the Other Side of Sorrow,* Edinburgh, 1995, p. 154

81 Lister-Kaye, John, Ill Fares The Land, *Scottish Natural Heritage,* 1994, p. 17

82 Smout, Chris, The Highlands and the Roots of Green Consciousness, 1750-1990, *Scottish Natural Heritage,* 1990, p. 8

83 Hunter, James, *On the Other Side of Sorrow,* Edinburgh, 1995, p. 160

84 SCU/RSPB, *Crofting and the Environment: A New Approach,* Broadford and Edinburgh, 1992

85 Hunter, James, *On the Other Side of Sorrow,* Edinburgh, 1995, p. 176

86 See, e.g. SCU/RSPB, *Crofting and the Environment: A New Approach,* Broadford and Edinburgh, 1992, para 3. 16. Also, see Hunter, James, *The Making of the Crofting Community,* Edinburgh, 1976, at p. 210 where he argues that the pattern of government aid to crofting betrays a lack of sociological and historical insight into the realities of crofting life. There should be more support for crofters' non-agricultural activities. See also Hunter, J., *Crofting Works - But it could and should work better,* Sabhal Mòr lecture, Skye, 1990, and Devine, T. M., & Finlay, R.. J., (Eds), *Scotland in the 20th Century,* Edinburgh, 1996, p. 158. The Land Reform Policy Group set up by the Government in October 1997 has, however, in its final paper, 'Recommendations for Action', January 1999, proposed that there

should be '... legislation to remove the existing requirements that grants to
crofters should be linked to agricultural production thereby allowing
assistance to be directed specifically at supporting rural development
rather than simply agricultural production', (para. 6. 2). It is to be hoped
that the tide has turned from the time ' ... when people are encouraged by
grants and subsidies to do things that are sometimes agriculturally absurd' -
Grant, James Shaw, *The Part-Time Holding - An Island Experience,*
The Arkleton Lecture, 1983, The Arkleton Trust, 1983, p. 16

87   BBC Landward, 6th September, 1992
88   MacEwan, John, *Who Owns Scotland?* Edinburgh, 1977, p. 24
89   Although, because temporary visitors were included in the 1981 census
     figure, this may have exaggerated the actual increase in the resident
     population
90   In an analysis carried out as part of the North West Demographic Survey
     in 1989, it was found that 31 per cent. of the houses in Assynt were
     holiday homes and a further 2 per cent. were vacant
91   Paragraph 30(2) of the *Rules of Procedure of the Crofters Commission*
92   BBC Landward, 6th September, 1992
93   *Assynt Crofters' Trust Papers*
94   *Assynt Crofters' Trust Papers*
95   *Assynt Crofters' Trust Papers*
96   *Am Bratach,* September, 1992, p. 2
97   *The Independent,* September, 1992
98   *The Scotsman,* 17th September, 1992
99   *West Highland Free Press,* 18th September, 1992
100 *The Scotsman,* 23rd September, 1992
101 *The Herald,* 23rd September, 1992
102 *The Scotsman,* 23rd September, 1992
103 *The Herald,* 24th September, 1992
104 *The Scotsman,* 23rd September, 1992
105 *The Herald,* 24th September, 1992
106 *Assynt Crofters' Trust Papers*
107 *The Herald,* 1st October, 199
108 *The Herald,* 1st October, 1992
109 *The Herald,* 1st October, 1992
110 *Press & Journal,* 1st October, 1992
111 *Assynt Crofters' Trust Papers*
112 MacCuish Donald J., & Flyn, Derek, *Crofting Law,* Edinburgh, 1990, p. 95
113 Section 6 (8) *Deer (Scotland) Act 1959*
114 Section 33 (3) *Deer (Scotland) Act 1959*
115 9th November, 1992
116 10th November, 1992
117 13th November, 1992
118 November, 1992
119 For a list of grievances offered by John MacKenzie as to Edmund Vestey's
     alleged policy on development of the Assynt Estate, the reader is referred to
     Cramb, Auslan, *Who Owns Scotland Now? The use and abuse of private land,*
     Edinburgh, 1996, p. 34-35. See also MacPhail, Isobel, One Year On, the Assynt
     crofters are starting to see the bigger picture, *The Crofter,* December, 1993
120 Section 12 (2) *1993 Consolidation Act*
121 6th November, 1992
122 2nd November, 1992
123 *Assynt Crofters' Trust Papers*

CHAPTER 3

• After the Purchase •

**Passion and euphoria have given way to the business
of good estate management**

The land had been won but this was only the beginning. The crofters now had to adjust to their new responsibilities. There was much to be done and the sirens of doom had already been at work. Neill Graham-Campbell of Finlayson-Hughes was quoted in *The Independent* as saying: "I should think the crofters in Assynt will live to regret buying the estate." He said that no one could manage a crofting estate and make money.[1]

At the first meeting of the steering group after the announcement of the success of the Trust, Bill Ritchie said that the group had served its purpose and that it was now time to organise the necessary meetings to agree the membership of the Board of Directors of the Trust, the membership qualifications for the Trust and the day to day administration of the Trust and the estate. Other matters which required urgent attention were the negotiation of the conditions of the SNH grant, ensuring that all the pledges were honoured (by the middle of February, all but two of the pledges had been collected), arranging bridging finance to cover any delay in collecting pledges in time for the date of entry (in the event there was no need to draw down on this facility) and arranging insurance for the estate.

An extraordinary general meeting of the Trust was held on 23rd January 1993 at which the articles of association of the Trust were approved and the Board of Directors was elected, consisting of, in addition to Allan MacRae and Bill

Ritchie who were co-opted directors, John MacKenzie from Culkein Drumbeg, Ian MacLeod from Achmelvich, Jimmy Kerr from Balchladich, Felicite Basu from Clachtoll, Aileen Kinnaird from Achnacarnin, Pat MacPhail from Clashmore, Donald King from Clashnessie, Donald MacKenzie from Culkein Stoer, Hughie Matheson from Drumbeg, John Blunt from Nedd (although he resigned shortly after), Michael Lord from Raffin, Ishbel MacAuley from Stoer and Derek MacLeod from Torbreck. It was agreed that there should be a maximum of seventeen Directors and a minimum of two. It was also agreed that any crofter who had purchased his croft under the right to buy provisions of the 1976 Act could sell his croft to the Trust, and thus become a crofting tenant again.[2]

The Board of Directors met after the extraordinary general meeting to discuss a very full agenda, including proposals for a management structure, the appointment of an executive and staff (including the important position of an estate factor, or crofting administrator) and the appointment of sub-groups to deal with specific estate matters. The meeting also discussed business proposals for the estate which had already been received, membership of various outside organisations such as the Scottish Landowners Federation, and a new logo for the estate. Eric Robson described the atmosphere at that meeting: "Passion and euphoria have given way to the business of good estate management."[3]

It was recognised that because the Board of Directors was elected on a township basis, this could lead to unwieldy and inflexible management, and might also create difficulty in reaching policy decisions. There was also the risk that confidentiality might be perceived by members of the Trust as being at risk of being compromised in relation to issues concerning such matters as croft tenancies if they were to be discussed at full Board meetings. Against this, of course, it was important that the concept of community management should not itself be compromised by any feelings that a 'clique' was running the Trust. So a devolved management structure was devised consisting of a three man Executive and Working Groups drawn from Board members. Trust policy decisions would be taken by the full Board, but based upon recommendations from the relevant Working Group. The Executive would deal with the day to day business of the Trust and the estate (apart from crofting matters) but would refer back to the Board for decisions on all policy matters.

On matters relating to crofting legislation and the day to day administration of routine crofting issues, it was proposed that there should be appointed a crofting administrator. Matters which were not of a routine nature, such as croft assignations outside the family and the sale of house sites, would be decided on by the Executive within policy guidelines set out by the Board. There would be a right of appeal from decisions of the crofting administrator to the Executive and from there to the full Board. It was considered important, however, that crofting matters should not be dealt with on an individual basis by the Board. Clearly, the person who was to fill the position of crofting administrator would be someone who could combine all the necessary administration skills and hold the confidence and respect of the crofters. This was a particularly sensitive role and the title of the position was chosen carefully.[4]

So far as the Working Groups were concerned, it was proposed that there should be three to cover land and natural resources, commercial and industrial matters, and tourism and recreation.

At a meeting of the Board of Directors on 17th February, Allan MacRae, Bill Ritchie and John MacKenzie were appointed as the Executive and Pat MacPhail was appointed as the first crofting administrator. Michael Lord was appointed to the role of Secretariat of the Trust. The three Working Groups were set up with immediate priorities for the Land and Natural Resources group to look after deer management and game control, for the Commercial and Industrial group to look into ways of realising the value of Torbreck House (with a view to being able to repay the Highland Prospect loan), and for the Tourism and Recreation group to look into fishing permits. As we shall see, it was not long before these groups began to look into many other issues and proposals for the estate.

The decision as to whether or not the Trust should join the Scottish Landowners Federation raised interesting issues. John MacKenzie, the Regional Chairman of the SLF, was to give the SLF view of the Trust's success: "The SLF view of the Assynt crofters' purchase was - 'well done people' - the management of that piece of ground has had a fairly chequered history in recent years - the crofters showed a remarkable unity and determination to go ahead and we congratulate them and wish them well."[5] The SLF Convener wrote a letter to *The Scotsman*, published on 9th December 1992, congratulating the Trust on its success and said that the SLF: "... genuinely looks forward to their application for membership of the federation. The SLF has already established a constructive dialogue with the Scottish Crofters Union. We very much hope that this new development will prove to be another step in fostering a fruitful relationship between crofters and landlords."[6] The SLF had written directly to the Trust inviting it to become a member. It is interesting to note that the letter from Mr Barlow referred to a relationship *between* (emphasis added) crofters and landlords. In the case of Assynt, of course, the crofters *were* landlords. A difference of approach or philosophy clearly still remained and while the Trust recognised that there were, undoubtedly, some common interests, the Trust considered that there were other aspects of the relationships within the SLF and between the SLF and other bodies with which the Trust would not want to be identified. And so the Board decided that the Trust should not become a member.

The Board then turned its attention to less serious, but nonetheless important issues. First, the estate was henceforth to be known as the 'North Assynt Estate'. Second, the Trust was in need of a visual symbol of its identity. From the very beginning, Bill Ritchie's letters sent out on behalf of the Trust had had a logo on them. Plain pieces of paper had, he felt, less impact. The logo he had used came from the clip art on his computer and showed a man ploughing with a horse drawn plough; a very obvious rural scene but, in Ritchie's estimation, a very bad one! Although it gave an image of working the land, it said nothing at all about crofting, certainly not about crofting in the 20th century. With the Trust now managing the estate, there was a need for an image, a logo which was readily recognisable. So a competition was organised to find such a logo. There were a number of entries and, interestingly, two featured the split rock at Clachtoll. The winner was Uwe Rieck from Durness. He described his logo as featuring the land - as he said: "... which, after all, this is all about." The split rock he said was shown as a land mark and as part of the land (although ironically, of course, the split rock was not, in fact, part of the estate - it was on land excluded from the original sale in 1989 and retained by the Assynt Estate). The bow of writing formed by the words 'Assynt Crofters' Trust' he described as symbolising two things: hope and achievement, shown by a rainbow, rising sun or an aura, and protection and shelter and care for the land underneath it.

As a further celebration of the purchase of the estate, and a small fund raising exercise, a commemoration plate made by Highland Stoneware Limited of Lochinver was offered in a limited edition of 50. Each ten inch plate was individually painted in free hand with a scene of the split rock and hand lettered 'Assynt Crofters' Trust 1993' at the top of the plate and with the words 'A' chlach sgoilt', the split rock, at the bottom. They sold for £45 each, and they were all taken up.

• The Trust and the individual crofter - a potential for conflict of interest or tension? •

The interaction between the individual crofter and the Trust as landlord raised new and interesting issues, something which was described by Bill Ritchie as the test of maturity of democracy. The crofter was now, in effect, his own landlord; but whereas the Trust (comprised of individual crofters) as landlord had the interests of the community (being all those individual crofters who were members of the Trust) as being its primary responsibility, the individual crofters could, quite properly, have their own individual interests in mind when running and taking decisions about their own crofts. And, of course, Trust policies are being made, and decisions being taken, by a group of individuals some of who may well have crofts in the same township, even a neighbouring croft, as the crofter affected by the Trust decision. There was, and is, a clear possibility of disputes and conflicts of interest arising. There is the possibility for 'tension between community development on the one hand and protecting the interests of individual crofters ...' on the other.[7] Furthermore, there was, and is, the likelihood that individual crofters might, in effect, blur the distinction between landlord and tenant, Trust and crofter, and consider themselves as owners of their crofts and entitled to do what they want without reference to the Trust.

The Trust as landlord has, under the Crofting Acts, rights whose exercise could bring the Trust as landlord, into conflict with an individual member of the Trust as a crofter.

To take some examples; a crofter is not entitled to open a
house on the croft for the sale of intoxicating liquor without
the consent of the landlord.[8] A crofter requires the consent
of the landlord to erect a dwelling house on the croft.[9] When
a croft becomes available for re-letting, it is the landlord who
is, in the first instance, responsible for the nomination of the
tenant and applications for the tenancy of the croft are made
to the landlord. Any township objections to the nomination
of a tenant by the landlord would be considered by the
Crofters Commission, but normally only when the landlord
has made the selection and applied to the Commission for
the tenancy to be granted. (We saw earlier in this Chapter
how the organisation of the administration of the Trust
had been designed to minimise problems arising in this area,
in particular by having township consultations before
submitting an application to the Commission, but even here
there has been an example of a difference of opinion
between the Trust and a township as to the selection of a new
tenant). There is an excess of applicants for crofts over the
availability of crofts and the choice of a new tenant raises
difficult issues, in particular the extent to which 'incomers' or
people who may not be felt to have that strong attachment to
the land which is typical of the native - that sense of *dùthchas*,
should be allowed into the townships.[10] A further example
might be if the Trust wanted to erect houses to further its
housing policy in the interests of the community, but where
the relevant township was not prepared to release the
necessary land. The Trust may take the view that it is in the
interests of the estate, and therefore of the members as a
whole, that a croft, in whole or part, or common grazings
should be resumed by the Trust for this purpose. These are
all areas where the Trust will make community decisions
which may, or may not, coincide with the wishes of the
individual crofter; where the Board members of the Trust

will be required to take decisions in the interests of the community and will be required to ignore their own personal interest in those decisions. In a memorandum to the Scottish Select Committee on the Transfer of Crofting Estates (Scotland) Bill (see Chapter 5) the Scottish Crofters Union summarised the position well: "The nature of crofting community activity is often subject to dispute, as in any situation where a considerable number of people must work together. At present if there is a dispute everyone is in the same position, and they know that their neighbours are not their landlord. Thus, there is resolution within the community, but the option remains to seek outside arbitration by landlord if appropriate. With a local community Trust your neighbour may hold an important position, and hence may have influence over the direction and use of the powers of land ownership. It is much easier to look at your landlord, and the power that represents, from a distance, but it creates much more tension if that power is your next door neighbour."[11]

There is, however, a crucial distinction to be made between the Trust as a landlord and the usual landlord of an estate which has crofting tenants, and that is that the Trust is a crofting landlord with a vision and a set of objective criteria for managing the estate in the interests of the crofting members and of the community. This could not necessarily, or at all, be said of any other Highland estate.[12] So a community policy could be devised under which decisions of the landlord, for example those required under the Crofting Acts, could be taken consistently in the interests of all the crofting members of that community. And it is worth remembering, in this context, that development value realised on a transaction is shared between the crofter and the landlord or the relevant grazings committee and the landlord; in the case of a crofting Trust, the landlord's share of the development value is, therefore, realised for the crofting community as a whole. There will, of course, be instances where individual crofters are upset by decisions of the Trust, but such crofters should, at least in theory, be comforted by the fact that the decisions are taken in the community interest rather than to forward any individual interest of the landlord and, crucially, any individual commercial interest of the landlord which may be competing with the commercial aspirations of those crofters.

• Trust projects •

We turn now to look, in brief, at how the Trust has begun, in the five years since the purchase, to develop the assets of the estate. The Trust wanted to return the value of the estate to the community, to seek to use the assets of the estate to retain the young people of the area and retain the support of the local population, to provide a new climate in which the local people would feel they were going to be encouraged to take part in enterprise which would bring employment to the community.

• Generation from renewable resources •

It was only to be expected, given the abundance of wind and water, that the Trust should consider at an early stage, whether and how these natural resources could be developed. In the first year after the purchase, the Trust had identified Loch Poll as a possible site for hydro electric generation and was also looking at the possibility of water generation at Clashnessie and wind generation at Stoer Head. While the idea of wind generation was shelved due to limitations imposed by the grid and the technical considerations of upgrading the line to Stoer Head, by the end of 1993 the Trust was taking advice from Dougall Baillie Associates of East Kilbride on possible schemes at Loch Poll and Clashnessie and had applied under the Scottish Renewables Order for both schemes to be registered. Loch Poll offered the greatest potential for generation due to the relatively large catchment area. There were, however, two potential problems. Neither the Loch itself nor part of the western bank of the Loch was in the ownership of the Trust and so the consent of the third party owner would have to be sought, and the level of the Loch would have to be raised by about two metres. So far as the Clashnessie site was concerned, all the relevant land was owned by the Trust, but there was a concern that the owners of holiday homes in the area might object to the reduction in water in the waterfall and to the erection of a small power house close by. In the event, however, it was not the holiday home owners who stopped the Clashnessie scheme but the crofters themselves. There was almost total opposition to the Clashnessie site from the Trust members in Clashnessie, and the plan to develop this site was abandoned; an interesting example of crofters and Trust wishes diverging. Some 190 organisations expressed an interest in supplying electricity to the two generators from renewable sources and after a detailed process of technical and financial scrutiny, the Office of Electricity Regulation awarded a 15 year contract to the Trust to supply 225kw of electricity to the grid. There were over 30 other successful bidders.[13]

Before work could start however, planning consent was required together with various other regulatory approvals and the negotiation of a funding package. We saw in Chapter 2 that the involvement of Scottish Natural Heritage in the Trust's bid for the estate exposed some important divisions within the steering group, particularly with regard to the influence which SNH might have in the running of the estate. The Loch Poll hydro scheme was to be a further example of the difficulties crofters and environmentalists still have over the management of land, whether these difficulties are real or perceived and the Loch Poll scheme was to result in the first formal vote the Trust had had. Because the plans would involve raising the level of the Loch, the Trust would be required to produce an environmental impact assessment to accompany the necessary planning application and the Trust consulted SNH on this, a consultation required irrespective of SNH's financial involvement in the Trust's bid for the estate. The Trust was told that SNH was statutorily obliged to do everything in its power to safeguard the blackthroated divers on the Loch as they were a protected species, and so SNH would object, at the planning stage, to the Trust's proposals. There then erupted in the press a public debate about the role of SNH, with less than complimentary comparisons being drawn between Lord Strathnaver who had been given an SNH grant of £100,000 for not destroying a forest on his estate, and the Assynt crofters who, apparently, SNH would not help financially to the tune of some £35,000 to alter the scheme to take account of the blackthroated divers.[14] John MacKenzie, in a letter to the *West Highland Free Press*, which complained bitterly about SNH's position, stated that: "... the problem is the legislative framework under which SNH operates and the perception by senior staff of their mandate from government."[15] He called for SNH to be brought under some form of public accountability. The chief executive of SNH, Roger Crofts, responded in the columns of the *West Highland Free Press* to the effect that SNH was still happy: "... to continue our dialogue with Assynt Crofters' Trust whose efforts we have supported and applauded ever since the Trust's inception."[16] And in the same issue, Kenny MacKenzie, the Trust's chairman, wrote that in fact, the Trust had abandoned the project due to the opposition of the other riparian owner and the prohibitive sums the Trust would have had to raise; something in the region of £100,000. He said that: "While SNH might ultimately have been a problem for us, nevertheless we had established a good working relationship with their personnel and appeared to be making some progress with them on a personal level. We had not, however, reached the point of full negotiations between their Board and ours."[17] And there matters rested for a while although the project had not, as suggested, been abandoned and funding for the project through Dennis Macleod, a mining entrepreneur who had been born and brought up in Helmsdale, went to South Africa and was now in Dingwall, had initially seemed assured.

New plans based on developments including the two smaller lochs to the south east of Loch Poll which would get round the problem of the water level in Loch Poll and the objections of the other riparian owner, together with a partnership with another company, Highland Light and Power, which would put up part of the development capital and manage the project for the Trust, with the aim being for the project to be given back, debt free, to the Trust at the end of a 15 year period, are close to a successful outcome. At the end of January 1999, Highland Council approved the plans and SNH and Scottish Environmental Protection Agency had withdrawn their objections. The plans mean that there should be some fifteen jobs produced during the construction phase and one full time position when production starts, and the Trust should benefit by some £200,000 over the life of the contract.[18]

• Native woodlands •

Trees and woodland were hugely important in Celtic culture and it is symbolically appropriate that the Gaelic alphabet was connected, for mnemonic purposes, with the names of trees. Trees often feature in the imagery employed by Gaelic poetry and tradition and woodlands were considered at great length in the Gaelic law tracts, reflecting their importance to the workings of the *tuath*[19] and we saw in Chapter 1 the importance of the *tuath* in the psyche of the Gael and, in particular, to his view of the land. In his early letters to opinion formers, Bill Ritchie had described woodland projects as one of the objectives of the Trust and from the outset it was Trust policy to encourage townships where possible to diversify into forestry, to explore its complimentary benefits to crofting of shelter for stock, timber and improvement of freshwater fisheries.[20] Throughout the estate, township houses were being built using local timber of some 100 years old from a plantation which was milled in Assynt. Replanting would secure supplies for the generations to come.

In April 1995 a Native Woodland Scheme of 162 hectares under the Crofters Forestry (Scotland) Act 1991 was begun on the Achmelvich common grazings in association with Tillhill Economic Forestry and with full Trust support. Tillhill were to carry out the work involving £250,000 over a 15 year period with Scotch pine, silver birch, hazel, oak, rowan, ash and alder being planted. The fencing of the hill ground commenced in the Autumn of 1995 and the planting took place during the winter of 1995-6. The woodland qualified under the Woodland Premium Scheme and so the shareholders in the common grazings would receive £6,000 per annum over the first 15 years to compensate them for putting the land over to forestry. The role of the Trust in the scheme was, first, as landlord to give the necessary statutory consent and, second, to provide administrative assistance. The financial benefits went to the crofters in the Achmelvich township, but the Trust was taking a proactive stance in encouraging other townships on the estate to follow suit and thus to allow an integrated approach to the planting of native woodlands on the estate as a whole. Since then, further schemes, each of around 120 hectares, have got under way. In Clachtoll and Stoer land is fenced and planted and interest has been expressed in most of the other townships. A small experimental planting is being carried out at Raffin and the preservation of existing woodlands, particularly in the Drumbeg area is being looked at.

• Fishing and Deer •

The land purchased by the Trust contains numerous lochs, both small and large and revenues from the sale of permits and the hire of boats has been a very important item of revenue for the Trust, far more, indeed, than the feasibility study and business plan had, in fact, anticipated and the Trust has achieved an annual income of some £6,000 from the sale of permits to fish at £5 a day. Development and improvement of the brown trout stock and loch fishing, pathways and signing, has continued since 1993 and 1995 saw the production of an attractive brochure giving details of the lochs with the most easy access accompanied by tempting descriptions: 'Loch Crocach - a particularly beautiful loch, with islands of preserved ancient woodland. Usually full of fish coming for the fly, it is ideal for learning about fishing, but also contains large fish.' And: 'Loch Cul Fraoich - a maddening loch. It can yield the very highest quality of trout ... these fish are of dark pink flesh, and of such a delicious flavour, that fishermen are driven back ... despite blank days.' There are 10 boats available for hire.

The Trust is also looking, in conjunction with the North West
Sutherland Fisheries Trust, at a programme for re-establish-
ing the sea trout and salmon migratory fishing system based
on the Manse Loch, and 50,000 salmon smolts were released
in the Oldany River in 1993 and, in 1998, 30,000 sea trout
fry were released into the Manse Loch system. These developments could create a number of seasonal jobs with the
possibility of at least one full time job.

Shooting for a number of stags and hinds on the estate is
let out to a local family together with the right to put boats
on one of the lochs and the tenant takes parties stalking and
fishing, but it is not the intention of the Trust that deer
management and stalking should become wholly operated
by third parties. Allan MacRae stresses that the Trust does
not regard itself as possessing a deer sporting estate; the
whole attitude to deer is different from that of the traditional
landlord. Deer are a wild animal which come onto croft
lands, destroy crops and compete on the grazings with
crofters' livestock. Marauding deer have always been seen as
a source of food. But the deer are also an asset of the estate
which the Trust will manage. A delicate balance is struck: "If
the sporting rights can be used for the benefit of the
community, good and well, but they won't be in competition
with the crofters."[21] And MacRae again: "There is no word
for 'poacher' in the Gaelic language. We may have people
who shoot more deer than they should. But we don't have
poachers." The contrast with the attitude of the traditional
Highland landlord is marked.

• Housing •

The creation of affordable house sites for local young people
was a key objective for the Trust from its inception and was,
and still is, regarded as a key element in demonstrating the

long term benefits of community ownership of crofting lands. But it was important that the new houses created went to the most deserving cases. In Bill Ritchie's words the Trust wanted to find ways of "... strategically targeting the housing to ensure it helps the people we want to assist and does not simply end up in the second homes and retirement market." The Trust began, at an early stage after the estate was purchased, talks with the national housing agency Scottish Homes with a view to grant aid being provided for individuals building new homes and with Sutherland District Council, Highland Regional Council and the North West Council of Social Services. Discussions centred on the possibilities of setting up a housing agency which would probably embrace an area greater than the estate. The Trust consulted with all the townships as to land on the estate which might be suitable for such housing and most of the townships expressed interest, and areas of the common grazing have been identified as suitable to be released for housing. Two possible sites have been identified at Stoer where the common grazings run alongside the road, thus making access much easier.[22]

• Croft Entrants Scheme •

This scheme, operated by the Crofters Commission in partnership with the Highlands and Islands Enterprise network (in the case of Assynt, CASE) encourages young people into crofting. It provides financial support, for work such as fencing and ditching, and guidance for new entrants and assists inactive crofters to release their crofts to young people. While the Trust has no firm role in relation to the Scheme, it has a policy that when crofts become vacant, new tenants should, where possible, be young people and some five or so new entrants have already been welcomed onto the estate.

• Croft holidays and tourism •

The Trust has successfully instituted a scheme with Aigas Field Centre in Beauly and Elder Hostel of the USA offering people from the United States the opportunity of seeing the crofting way of life through on-croft holidays. Since 1996 some 30 or so people have participated each year in the scheme and have been provided with bed and breakfast accommodation on crofts in estate townships, taken part in croft activities such as sheep management and fishing, and been taken on visits to historic and other interesting sites in the area. While the main income from the scheme has gone to the crofters participating in the scheme, the Trust receives a lump sum from the organisers to promote the scheme, and so it is income earning for the Trust. Further projects are being examined to encourage tourism in the area for the benefit of the townships and, in particular, to devise a strategy for tourism.[23]

• Telematics •

Torbreck Lodge (which had been let to Implex Environmental Systems shortly after the Trust took over the estate) was sold by the Trust in 1995 to Implex, which had, in fact, exercised an option to purchase. This was a move which enabled the Trust to repay, in full, the £90,000 loan from Highland Prospect. Implex is a Liverpool based company which was a pioneer in the development of computer software for environmental monitoring and emergency response systems for local authorities, fire brigades and emergency planning units across the country, and which measures background radiation and toxic gas levels and meteorological parameters at over 80 sites throughout the United

Kingdom. A summary of all this information is fed into Implex's computer system at Torbreck Lodge. Implex has provided employment for two young local people, allowing them to learn new skills.

The Trust is seen as being keen to operate on a basis of sustainable development and environmental sensitivity and the practical significance of this is demonstrated by the involvement of the Trust, together with another land manager, CEAM (a forestry research group in Valencia, Spain) and two industrial partners, Implex and Software AG Espana of Madrid in a project known as STEM (or sustainable telematics for environmental management). The project, which has EU funding, is assessing the feasibility of developing a practical application of computer technology to aid land and environmental management with geographic information systems, remote data handling and the use of local knowledge. The aim is to take advantage of the possibilities of this technology in a way that makes it useful to crofters who are trying to manage and develop their land, grazings or the whole estate. In Assynt, the project is concentrated on gathering data about Loch Poll. The project is being coordinated by the University of Edinburgh's Department of Artificial Intelligence and the Human Communication Research Centre, and involves academics from CWI in Amsterdam and the University of Karlsruhe in Germany. It is a good example of how the Trust is making use of its resources in an inventive, forward looking way. The involvement of the Trust with such bodies gives it wider recognition outside the UK as an exciting and innovative area of rural development. It has, for example, led to the Trust being involved with the World Wild Life Fund for Nature, Energy Unlimited and Stirling University in a project examining energy demand and identifying options for renewable energy systems. The Trust has also been approached by a Dutch company which is looking into the possibilities for rural communities to feed 'green' electricity into the grid.

• Other •

In most areas the Trust sees its role as being a facilitator for the townships to take advantage of the various opportunities which are available. The Trust is looking into the possibilities of putting together a fund which can be drawn on by townships to assist with the cash that must be raised by crofters for such matters as fencing, which can involve large sums even after grants and subsidies are taken into account. It is also looking at the possibilities of developing native plants for alternative medicine; again, it would be the individual crofters who would, if interested, take advantage of any such scheme.

The Trust already makes a small financial surplus on the management of the estate despite the fact that anticipated major flows of revenue (from, for example, the hydro-electric project) have not yet materialised. The financial surplus is not, however, sufficient to support a number of projects which could develop the economic potential of the Trust's assets and funding for these projects has to be found elsewhere. John MacKenzie also believes that the experiences of the first five years of the Trust have shown that it will be important to look at projects which are not directly related to land use, or at least to non-agricultural production.

There are sceptics, both within and outside of the Trust and it is seen as crucial to the success of the Trust that the crofters on the estate are themselves active. As a senior member of the Trust has said: "Crofters must put their own efforts into the running of the estate; they cannot just sit back and expect the Trust to deliver a crock of gold." The responsibilities and burdens in running an estate on behalf of a community are heavy. The voluntary nature of the work undertaken by the officers and committee members of the Trust means that it is very important that a sense of purpose, a sense of community backing is maintained. Without it, the willingness of individuals in the administration of the Trust will falter.

• I am not sure they have anything they hadn't got already, apart from being able to say they own the land •

We end this Chapter with a review of some of the perceptions of what the Assynt crofters felt they had achieved and of their feelings for the land, and contrast them with what might be described as a traditional Highland landlord's view.

We take, first, the words of Allan MacRae: "Walking across my croft and looking at my sheep gives me a satisfaction that money can't buy. I do feel emotionally attached to the land and I know every bit of it round here. I can visualise the whole croft in my mind. One's feelings about the land are the same as those of indigenous people all over the world. In the Highlands, people talk about what we did as radical, but it's not. Maybe in terms of Highland history, but not in terms of human history, that's the important thing. The most natural thing in the world is that a community such as ours should own the land; the only unnatural thing that happened in Assynt was that we had to pay £300,000 for something that should really have belonged to us. You can go to many parts of the world and you will find indigenous peoples like ourselves seeking to retain control of their land, indeed seeking to repossess lands

that they have been dispossessed of in the past. There's
nothing unique in what we are doing. Nothing whatsoever. I
think it's just something very basic to human nature."[24]
MacRae's references to indigenous peoples draws parallels
between the crofters' claim for land restitution and that of
Africans, native Americans and Aboriginals,[25] and Eric
Robson on the BBC Landward programme 'Lights in the
Glen'[26] portrayed MacRae's passionate beliefs as finding
resonances in ethnic struggles elsewhere. In October 1996
the Scottish Crofters Union wrote to the Government asking
for crofters to be recognised as an indigenous people with
the same rights as the Maoris of New Zealand and the
Australian Aborigines, a claim the legal basis of which was
supported by Glasgow University. "A strong argument can
be made that crofters are an indigenous people, because
their people have always been on the land, they have a
different culture and, in some places, the distinct Gaelic
language."[27] But care must be taken, in making such claims,
not to fall into the trap of inferiorisation. For centuries the
Gael was labelled as wild and uncivilised. The notorious
Patrick Sellar believed the language of the Highlander to be
an 'obstinate adherence to the barbarous jargon of the times
when Europe was possessed by Savages' and the fact that
they excluded themselves from the 'grand fund of
knowledge' of Europe, '... placed them, with relation to the
enlightened nations of Europe in a position not very different
from that betwixt the American Colonies and the Aborigines
of that Country.' The Highlanders were, for Sellar, the
'Aborigines of Britain.'[28]

MacRae has some uncomfortable words for crofters:
"Maybe we have got to stop thinking like crofters. Crofting
is something of a mental straitjacket, conditioned by history
and not something easily thrown off ... Crofters have a hard
job to see beyond their security of tenure; they don't seem to

realise that maybe there could be a whole dimension beyond that ... in terms of land and rural development. I think that it is because crofters have had to struggle so hard for their rights ... that they find it difficult to look outside. Crofting is surrounded by land that is in the stranglehold of sporting landlords. So in a sense maybe they feel they are on a kind of offensive all the time defending what they have, and it is very hard to change that."[29] Allan MacRae, then, reveals some interesting insights. Running through his words there may, perhaps, be seen a sense of the inferiorisation which the Gael has suffered over the centuries.[30] But, more importantly, there is also a strong pointer towards the crofters taking responsibility for their own affairs, of breaking free from being prisoners of the past and of having the courage to think about developing crofting for the benefit of the community, of breaking free from an institutionalised system. MacRae's comments about a mental straitjacket and of the possibilities of land and rural development are particularly interesting because the fundamentals of crofting originally enshrined in the 1886 Act and which are, of course, still to be found at the centre of the current Crofting Acts, were subjected to some fairly searching criticism at the time of the centenary of the 1886 Act along these lines[31] and the Act has been criticised as being a force for conservatism, condemning crofting to inertia and stagnation.[32] Also the system created by the 1886 Act has been criticised as militating against leadership and innovation in both agricultural development and in the industrial and commercial pursuits which are part of crofting life.[33] MacRae clearly has a sense of belief in the future of the land; a sense of pride in what has been achieved; a positive outlook which is challenging the inferiorisation. He challenges the idea that crofters taking on responsibility for their lands is ground breaking. He sees it as the most natural thing in the world. But crofters must be proactive. "Communities" MacRae says "rather than wait for change to be thrust upon them have got to shape that change. And that is what we are trying to do in Assynt."[34]

In the BBC Landward programme that came back to Assynt a year after the purchase, Eric Robson, speaking to John MacKenzie, said that he had the feeling that there had been a spiritual change in the community. MacKenzie agreed that was a way of putting it; he suggested, for his part, that it was more, perhaps, a sudden sense of freedom. John MacKenzie sees an increased optimism in Assynt and, reflecting Allan MacRae's point, an enhanced resolve to engage in economic development, in areas which are totally removed from what normal crofting really means. We have already seen this in some of the projects in which the Trust is involved. He felt that representatives of the traditional Highland landowners were bemused by what the Assynt crofters were doing and why they wanted to do it. What more could they possess other than the title to the land? Certainly not the use of the land as, such people thought, they already had almost complete freedom. But MacKenzie points out that such people have lost sight of the intrinsic value to those who live and work on the land of having title to the land.

There were a number of interviews with Edmund Vestey in the aftermath of the success of the Assynt crofters. He spoke of his feelings for the land, as to what the success of the Trust meant, and it has to be said that the contrast between what we have seen, for example, Allan MacRae and John MacKenzie saying and what Edmund Vestey said in those interviews suggests a vast gap in understanding. When asked for his views on the success of the Trust, Vestey said: "It is an interesting experiment. I am not sure they have anything they hadn't got already, apart from being able to say they own the land. They had the grazing rights, and the ability to buy their own croft. They are able to say they are proud owners, but it has cost them quite a lot of money to achieve that. They had everything except the title to the land."[35] Cramb says, in his book, that there appears, in Vestey's comments, a lack of commitment to preserving community life. For MacRae and MacKenzie, of course, it is all about community matters. Cramb says that the view of the local residents of Assynt is that while Vestey: "... may love the place [it is] only as an oil painting, hunting ground, and salmon reservoir. Not as a place where people live and work, and may have aspirations for new development and opportunity."[36] The contrast between this and MacRae's thoughts as to the prospects for development of land for community purposes is marked indeed.

But perhaps more fundamental is the apparent failure to understand why it was that ownership of the estate was such an important goal for the Assynt crofters, the apparent failure to understand the depth of the sense of achievement which the crofters felt, and why. Failures which betray a frightening lack of understanding of the historical context. Asked by Eric Robson in the BBC Landward programme: "... when they talk about reversing the trend of 200 years of history, of getting back the land that is rightfully theirs. Did you take exception to this?" Vestey responded with a smile: "No. It's a nice sort of thought isn't it?"[37] It was, and is, far more than just a nice sort of thought.

Notes

1 *The Independent*, 12th December, 1992
2 The extent to which this would be possible would depend on whether the croft had been decrofted
3 Speaking in BBC Landward, transmitted in November, 1993
4 It is interesting that the term 'crofting administrator' rather than the more familiar 'factor' with its associations with unhapy landlord/crofter relationships, was used
5 Speaking in, *An e Farmad a nì Treabhadh?* Grampian TV, transmitted on 13th December, 1993
6 N. R. D. Barlow, *The Scotsman*, 9th December, 1992
7 *SSC Evidence*, para 189
8 Paragraph 12, Schedule 2, *1993 Consolidation Act*
9 Paragraph 8, Schedule 2, *1993 Consolidation Act*
10 See Jedrej C., and Nuttall M., *White Settlers - The Impact of Rural Repopulation in Scotland*, Luxembourg, 1996, pp. 161-165 and 175-181
11 *SSC Evidence*, page 46
12 Apart, of course, from The Stornoway Trust and those estates which have, since the Assynt example, become community estates
13 Source: *Assynt Crofters' Trust Newsletter*, No 1
14 See, for example, *West Highland Free Press*, 18th April, 1997
15 18th April, 1997
16 18th April, 1997
17 18th April, 1997
18 See *Am Bratach*, February, 1999
19 Hunter, James, *On the Other Side of Sorrow*, Edinburgh, 1995, p. 61-62
20 For a description of native woodland management in North West Sutherland, see Sheridan, Andrew, Native Woodland Management and expansion in the far North East, in Mollison, Denis, (ed), *Sharing the Land*, John Muir Trust, 1994
21 Allan MacRae quoted in *The Herald*, 1st February, 1992
22 See *Am Bratach*, January, 1999
23 It might be noted that there are potential dangers in the encouragement of cultural tourism, of, perhaps, seeing the culture of the crofting area as a product or a commodity. See, for example, Gaelic: A Future for the Heritage, by Donald E. Meek in *Aberdeen University Review*, LVII, No 197, Spring 1997, pp. 13-18 and Jedrej, C., and Nuttall, M., *White Settlers - The Impact of Rural Repopulation in Scotland*, Luxembourg, 1996, pp. 83-87. But see Macdonald, Sharon, A People's Story-Heritage, identity and authenticity, in Rojeck, C., and Urry, J., (eds) *Touring Cultures - Transformations of Travel and Theory*, London, 1997, pp. 155-175 which discusses the commodification of culture and history in the context of the Aros centre in Skye.
24 Speaking on BBC Landward, transmitted on 6th September, 1992
25 McIntosh, Alastair, Wightman, Andy, and Morgan, Daniel, Reclaiming the Scottish Highlands - Clearance, Conflict and Crofting, in *The Ecologist*, vol 24, No 2, 1994, p. 68
26 Transmitted 6th September, 1992
27 Catriona Drew quoted in *The Daily Telegraph*, 11th October, 1996
28 Adams, R. .J., *Papers on Sutherland Esate Management*, Edinburgh, 1972, volume 1, p. 175-6

29 Speaking on BBC Landward, transmitted in November, 1993

30 For a discussion of the concept of inferiorisation in the Highland context, see Hunter, James, *On the Other Side of Sorrow,* Edinburgh, 1995, pp. 28-39 and the works quoted there

31 See, for example, Macinnes, Allan, The Crofters Holdings Act of 1886: A Hundred Year Sentence? *Radical Scotland* No 25, Feb/Mar, 1987

32 Devine, T. M., *Clanship to Crofters' War - The social transformation of the Scottish Highlands,* Manchester and New York, 1994, p. 234

33 Caird, J. B., and Moisley, H. A., Leadership and Innovation in the Crofting Communities in the Outer Hebrides, *Sociological Review*, ix, 1961, p. 87 and 88

34 Speaking on BBC Landward transmitted in November, 1993

35 Quoted in Cramb, Auslan, *Who Owns Scotland Now? The use and abuse of private land,* Edinburgh, 1996, p. 44. See also MacPhail, Isobel, One Year on, the Assynt crofters are starting to see the bigger picture, *The Crofter,* December, 1993

36 Cramb, Auslan, *Who Owns Scotland Now? The use and abuse of private land,* Edinburgh, 1996, p. 35

37 Speaking on BBC Landward, transmitted in November, 1993

CHAPTER 4

The Role of the Press
and the Media

• Introduction •

The Highlander, and in particular the crofter, will not be a stranger to the role the press and the media have played in 19th century Highland affairs. During the famine years after 1846, it is said that newspaper campaigns directly contributed to a decreasing amount of sympathy and charity for the Highlanders and further strengthened Lowland prejudices against their Highland neighbours.[1] In particular, it is said, there was a vitriolic campaign to this effect in *The Scotsman* and in pamphlet literature.[2] The Highlander was portrayed as lazy, idle, indolent, neglectful, inherently slothful, ignorant and dirty. The lazy Highlander was taking advantage of the charity and benevolence of the industrious Lowlander. This campaign played a part in the radical changes which took place in the famine relief system in the Highlands after 1848. But these views were not expressed by all the press, and journals such as the *North British Daily Mail* and *The Inverness Advertiser* argued just as strongly that even more liberal aid and support was required by the Highlands.

During the years of the Crofters' War in the 1880s, the role of the press and journals in publishing the concerns of the crofters and the incidents which took place, was very important. Newspapers and journals which showed an interest in the problems of the crofters multiplied in the 1880s and more space was devoted to the Highlands and Islands by the older established newspapers.[3] Papers such as the *North British Daily Mail, The Oban Times* and *The Inverness*

Advertiser were sympathetic to, and championed for, the crofters' cause while *The Times, The Scotsman* and *The Inverness Courier* were firm supporters of landlords and farmers, but even they did not draw back from giving publicity through the reporting of news of, and writing articles about, the crofters' struggles, and published the speeches on the important issues.[4] And, of course, John Murdoch's paper *The Highlander* and *The Celtic Magazine* and *An Gaidheal* played vital roles and helped to articulate the crofters' feelings.

While in the closing years of the 20th century the press and the media generally now play a far more prominent and, some would say, a dangerously formative, even pivotal, role in society, and thus might have been expected to be a significant element in the campaign of the Assynt crofters, what might not, perhaps, have been expected was the almost wholesale sympathy and support which they gave to the crofters, even from *The Scotsman*.[5] But in his book, *The Claim of Crofting*, James Hunter writes that crofters are favourably regarded by the Scottish people, if, perhaps, somewhat sentimentally and romantically.[6] Why this is so is, he says, a complex subject but he suggests that, at its simplest, it may be because of a "... widespread feeling that crofters have had an extremely raw deal from history."[7] The role of the media during the campaign by the Assynt crofters was, without doubt, to exploit this sympathy and to do so, in large part, by dwelling on the sentimental and romantic aspects and, in particular, the dark years of the late 18th century and the 19th century.

The press and media coverage of the purchase of the North Lochinver Estate can conveniently be divided into two kinds: background articles and comment, and factual reporting of events and developments.

• Background articles and comment •

In the main, the background articles and comment looked at the historical backdrop to the purchase, at the clearances, the years of the Crofters' War, and drew attention to how these turbulent years in the Highlands had affected Assynt. A number of them also concentrated on the role of the Vestey family in Assynt. Many such articles were pure polemic and unashamedly colourful and emotional in their descriptive passages of the empty straths and townships, of overbearing landlords, of '... remnants of population huddled by the shore while the huge hinterland lies empty', of crofting townships clinging to a spectacular coastline, of how Assynt was once given by an English Duke to his prospective son in law as a wedding present as others might give a tea service. There was no doubt where the sympathies of this reporting lay. References to a meat enriched Vestey family keeping a tight reign on any development not approved of, to the iron grip of the Vesteys, to stories about 20th century life in Assynt not being out of place in the context of evidence given to the Napier Commission, all gave a clear and unequivocal message.

The campaign by the Assynt crofters was also the ideal opportunity to advance the long felt desires of a number of people radically to overhaul the system of landownership in the Highlands and to find a new way forward for crofting. And so, in addition to articles and comment reminding the readers of the dark years of 19th century Highland history and the continuing evils of Highland sporting landlords, a number of articles were published suggesting that the move by the Assynt crofters marked, if not the start of a revolution towards community ownership throughout the seven crofting counties, then a new phase in this revolution. James Hunter made this point very clearly, but, just in case it was thought that the move by the Assynt crofters was the "... first step on a road likely to lead inexorably to the red flag being hoisted over Dunrobin Castle," Hunter, writing in *The Scotsman*, made the point that the idea of community ownership should not necessarily be seen as a creature of left wing politics, but that it also made good sense from a number of different perspectives.[8] The historical significance of what the Assynt crofters were doing was emphasised by these background articles and comment. James Hunter believed that 1992 might, some 200 years after the infamous *Bliadhna nan Caorach* - the Year of the Sheep, come to be remembered as the Year of the Assynt Crofter: "A lot of us have been, for a long time, nurturing a dream ... a dream that has never quite lost its power to inspire. It's a dream that the land from which so many of our folk were once expelled will one day belong, not to the lairds and property companies and government departments, certainly not to London liquidators acting on behalf of foreign banks ... but to people like the men and women who have organised the Assynt Crofters' Trust."[9] In a leading article in *The Scotsman*, published on the day after the announcement of the Trust's success[10] prominence was given to the vision of George Campbell, the Director of the Scottish Crofters' Union, who believed that the success of the Trust could presage a change in the whole pattern of land ownership. The crucial point for him was, so the article described, that the investment on estates in community ownership could filter down for the benefit of the people living on the estate.

David Ross, writing in *The Herald*,[11] saw the move by the Assynt crofters as nothing less than a direct challenge to the fundamentals of property ownership in the Highlands: "It is difficult to overstate the importance of the current campaign by 100 Sutherland crofters to buy the land on which they live on the North Lochinver Estate. There is a great deal more riding on it than just the future of 21,000 acres of crofting land in and around the Stoer Peninsula. The private ownership of Highland land has been an emotive issue for so long that the debate has become sterile. Few outside the estate owners themselves really believe the maintenance of human deserts or the ownership of communities can be right. There have been good landlords, some very good, but even they could never be completely disassociated from the immorality of the clearances which carved out their estates, and that perhaps is a shame. But to challenge such a fundamental as property rights was always seen as something only the powers of government could undertake."

And *The Inverness Courier*, that steadfast supporter of landlords in the Crofters' War wrote, in a leading article on 15th September, the day before the final closing date for offers for the estate: "If you have not been following what has been going on of late in [Assynt], you may not realise just how significant Wednesday 16th September 1991 could turn out to be in the chequered history of land tenure in the Highlands ... The hope now must be that their attempt to secure title of the land, and thereby secure the future of their shattered community, will be looked on kindly. The crofters, we believe, deserve to have control of the soil from which so many families were evicted during the heartless Clearances of the last century. There would be a certain justice in it."[12] In its leading article celebrating the Trust's success, the same newspaper ended by saying: "There can be no doubt in anyone's mind that the Assynt Trust's triumph has loosened the grip of private landowners in the North and placed crofting on the threshold of a new and exciting era."[13]

Articles such as these helped to establish that something of not just historic importance but also of current social importance was happening in Assynt.

But it was not just the written media which carried such

background and comment. The BBC Landward programme 'Lights in the Glen' was, as the pages of this account have shown, an influential piece of broadcasting presented by Eric Robson some two weeks before the first closing date for offers for the estate. The programme looked at the issues of landownership in the Highlands, at the lack of settled community populations, at forestry issues. But, again, there was no doubt where the sympathies of the programme lay. It began with a memory of the Clearances, with Eric Robson speaking in the graveyard at Croick where Highlanders who had been cleared from Glencalvie had huddled for shelter.[14] Criticism of the way the Highlanders had been treated over the years was implicit throughout and at times explicit: "More care would have been taken if it had been a rare plant or a bird of prey, than the care given to the inhabitants of the glen." Verse from Norman MacCaig's poem, 'A Man in Assynt' was read over evocative film of the scenery and, in particular, of Suilven, to emphasise the desolation. (Ironically, of course, it also showed the beauty of isolation which some would wish to preserve.) The programme referred to the 28th July meeting of the Assynt crofters at Stoer School as: "A meeting they hoped would do nothing less than change the course of Highland landownership." Interviews with, among others, Bill Ritchie, Allan MacRae and John MacKenzie gave full publicity to the hopes and the aims of the crofters. The message of the programme so far as the Assynt crofters were concerned was clear - setting the record straight. John MacKenzie described what they were doing as something which redressed the balance. Eric Robson asked MacKenzie whether it could be described as: "... getting your own back on the landlords?" MacKenzie replied: "... not by any means. It is our seeking to achieve what we consider to be our historical right." Was it, then: "... taking back what was taken from from you in the first place?"

and MacKenzie replied, "Precisely that."

The programme referred to the contingency plan of using the right to buy provisions of the crofting legislation. The significance of the Whitbread decision was made clear and the views of Highland landlords on this, through an SLF spokesman, examined. Robson described Highland landlords as watching the Assynt crofters' move to acquire the estate with interest and some trepidation. Could Assynt be the first domino to fall in a wave of crofter purchases? The Assynt crofters were described as raising their standard at a time when the traditional Highland landlords were in retreat. James Hunter said that the traditional estates were in serious trouble and the question was, what was to be put in their place? In certain areas there was, Hunter thought, and as we have seen, the potential to repopulate in a sensitive way. The programme finished, powerfully, with James Hunter talking about the fallacy of the wilderness theory which we described, in brief, in Chapter 2, and of the lights in the glen coming back on. There can be little doubt that this was an important and influential piece of reporting and its timing was highly significant.

And, in the way of the press, the key figures in the Assynt crofters' movement were given national prominence. Bill Ritchie was portrayed as the brains behind the Trust's purchase of the estate; an Edinburgh born man who had studied law at Oxford, but an 'incomer' of some 20 years, the classic multi-talented crofter. Allan MacRae, described by one journalist as a fierce bantam of a man, was portrayed as providing the passion to the campaign and certainly the passionate and articulate interviews he gave to the media, both written and visual, were enormously significant in giving the campaign its prominence. In this age of the sound bite, Allan MacRae's words provided many very forceful quotations with significant effect - as the pages of this account have shown. The fact that his great grandfather had been part of the clearances gave him, in the eyes of the media, added credibility.[15] John MacKenzie was described as providing the voice of conscience of the Assynt crofters. An engineer who had come back to Assynt after a career in Glasgow, to the land his family had known for generations, he spoke with quiet but firm assurance of the rationale behind the Trust. Others too were given prominence by the press.

The media visited Assynt again a year after the purchase. BBC Landward produced another programme presented by Eric Robson in November 1993. After a review of what had happened in Assynt, Robson looked at what the Trust was then doing, stressing that new opportunities had to be found to halt the decay. The contrast between the pictures of activities on the land and the activities of Implex at Torbreck Lodge gave striking visual emphasis to this point. As Robson said: "In this room the conversation would once have been of the stalking and the price of sheep. Today it is the whisper of electronics monitoring a chemical spill in the West Midlands, predicting a plume of toxic gas in some corner of urban Britain ..." Robson spoke to Edmund Vestey (and we have noted their exchanges elsewhere in this account), and ended by wondering what had happened to the spark of protest which it had been thought the Assynt crofters would set alight all the Highlands. What was holding back other crofters from following Assynt - was it nervousness or lack of interest? The special circumstances that had existed in Assynt would, he thought, be most unlikely to be duplicated elsewhere, but the idea of community ownership and community responsibility had been firmly sown and, in time, would produce results.

Grampian Television covered very similar ground in Great Day at Split Rock transmitted in 1993, but ended with some of the local children talking about their hopes for the future. Isabel Fraser, the presenter, summed up: "The young people are part of a community which has grown in stature and confidence, part of a radical movement that could halt the social erosion which has beset the Highlands for more than a century, and belong to a place where people control their destiny." A short programme presented by Forbes McFall for BBC Reporting Scotland, 'Making the Land Work', also looked at what the Trust was doing on the estate.[16]

The Gaelic programme produced by Grampian Television on 13th December 1993, whose theme was 'who owns the land?', was interesting. Assynt featured, but interviews were conducted with crofters from Bernera, Borve and Annishadder and Glendale in Skye. Crofters from Borve and Annishadder explained why they had followed the Assynt example, but different views were also put forward. A land agent emphasised the potential downside of community ownership by crofters - that all they were doing was putting themselves in line to pay bills formerly paid by estate owners.[17] Another landlord remarked that "crofters have understood the value of having something without the ownership."[18] The point was made that in a number of estates the crofters were perfectly happy with their landlords and did not see the estate producing the income to make it worthwhile for the crofters to consider community ownership, even if the estate was given to the crofters. Assynt was seen by one crofter as being poles apart from Bernera. And a crofter from Glendale spoke with a certain bitterness about what had happened there. The crofters had achieved ownership of the estate in 1956, but crofters had taken advantage of the demand for land from incomers and white settlers to the detriment, he believed, of the community. He earnestly hoped that what had happened in Glendale would not happen in Assynt. It was by no means the case that the Assynt example would find favour in other crofting townships.

• Reporting on events and developments •

From the outset, the steering group recognised the importance of a carefully managed media campaign given, in particular, the major strategy which was to discourage rival bidders and while the Trust did not have an official PR agency looking after its interests, it did, as was noted in chapter 2, receive considerable help and support from a number of journalists and 'unofficial' advice as to how to handle a media campaign. John MacKenzie recalls that the representatives of the media were, by and large, sympathetic and enthusiastic towards the cause. Some of them were themselves Highlanders and thus, more than most, conscious of the historical background.

The first reports of the moves by the Assynt crofters followed the issue of the press release by the Assynt Branch of the SCU on 9th June. The article by Jenny Shields in *The Daily Telegraph* of 1st July under the headline 'Crofters Gather to Plan Clearance of Landlords' in which she wrote of the challenge by Highlanders of traditional land ownership patterns and, in particular, of the significance of the Whitbread case, was considered by John MacKenzie to be the seminal event in terms of the start of the campaign and from then until February 1993, hardly a week went by without the campaign of the crofters receiving a mention in the press. As we have seen in chapter 2, each of the major events was given significant press coverage from, principally, *The Herald*, the *Press and Journal*, the *West Highland Free Press*, *The Northern Times*, the *Inverness Courier*, *The Independent*, *The Guardian* and *The Daily Telegraph*, and the monthly magazine *Am Bratach*. The reporting included quotations from, in the main, Allan MacRae, Bill Ritchie and John MacKenzie on behalf of the Trust and from other leading figures who were involved either directly or indirectly, and much of the proceedings of the important meetings of the crofters in Stoer School was reported verbatim.[19]

But not all the reporting was viewed as fair to the Assynt crofters. One particular report caused concern to the extent, indeed, that the Trust considered approaching the Press Ombudsman. This was the article in *Scotland on Sunday* on 7th February 1993 under the headline, 'Step We Gaily at the Assynt Victory Cèilidh'. The article reported on the celebration cèilidh and it was thought by some in Assynt that it portrayed the cèilidh as a drunken orgy. The *Assynt News*[20] believed that the article "romanticised the facts" and took poetic licence to its limits. It also criticised the article for its factual accuracy - in particular references to Torbreck Lodge as having been the "mansion owned and used by successive landlords". The Lodge was, in fact, a small house which had housed various estate staff over the years. But the Trust had benefited enormously from articles in the press which dwelt on the historical injustices which had been handed out to Highlanders over the years and, viewed objectively, this article was one more such article, no more and no less.

There can be little doubt that the press and media coverage had two principal effects. First, it encouraged a wave of sympathy for the cause of the crofters which lent considerable support to the fund raising efforts of the Trust. Second, to the extent that there were other parties interested in purchasing all or part of the estate, it had the effect of discouraging them and there is anecdotal evidence to this effect. A conversation between a lady who was interested in buying a Highland estate and the receptionist at a firm of land agents was overheard. In response to the question as to whether the firm knew of any such estates for sale, the prospective purchaser was told of the North Lochinver Estate. She immediately responded with the comment that she wanted nothing to do with that particular estate - was that not the one which was having all that trouble with the crofters?

The media coverage which revisited Assynt a year after the purchase and which looked at the issues of landownership in the Highlands, reminded the Assynt crofters that they and their successes and failures would not escape the limelight. The media had played a vital part in the success of the Trust in purchasing the estate and the Assynt crofters would not be allowed to leave the stage of public scrutiny. It also served to emphasise the particular circumstances which had existed in Assynt and that while the success of the Assynt crofters may have lit a beacon, the result would be more likely to stimulate debate about landownership in the Highlands, to encourage an overall change in attitudes to landownership[21] and, in particular, community ownership, than a wave of replica purchases throughout the Highlands.

Notes

1   *West Highland Free Press,* 11th November, 1994, p. 7, 'How the Scottish
    Press Waged War on the Highland Poor'
2   Devine, T.M., *Clanship to Crofters' War - The social transformation of the
    Scotthish Highlands,* Manchester and New York. 1994, p. 168
3   Macphail, I.M.M., *The Crofters' War,* Stornoway, 1989, p. 10
4   Macphail, I.M.M., *The Crofters' War,* Stornoway, 1989, p. 11
5   Although it should be noted that John MacKenzie does not believe that
    the attitudes of *The Scotsman* on this are markedly different from those of
    the 19th century newspaper
6   Hunter, James, *The Claim of Crofting,* Edinburgh, 1991, p. 18
7   Hunter, James, *The Claim of Crofting,* Edinburgh, 1991, p. 19
8   *The Scotsman,* 7th August, 1992
9   *Press & Journal,* 6th October, 1992
10 9th December, 1992
11 16th October, 1992
12 15th September, 1992
13 *Inverness Courier,* 11th December, 1992
14 Prebble, John, *The Highland Clearances,* London, 1969, pp. 218-225
15 He was the subject of a lengthy profile in the November 1992 edition of
    Am Bratach (p. 7)
16 Transmitted in November, 1993
17 Neil Graham-Campbell of Finlayson Hughes
18 Dr Laing speaking in the programme
19 See, for example, the *West Highland Free Press* report of the 20th June
    meeting in its 26th June, 1992 edition
20 12th February, 1993
21 This was reflected in the words of Andy Wightman in his address to the
    1995 SCU Conference: "Now Assynt was a watershed in the public
    perception of the land debate. It focussed people's attentions on the fact
    that it was possible for ordinary people to achieve change and it was
    instrumental in bringing land ownership back onto the political agenda."
    Am Bratach, February, 1996 p. 15. We shall look further at this in Chapter 5

CHAPTER 5

Crofting Trusts and the
Land Debate

• The first crofting Trust and early moves
towards community ownership of croft land •

The Assynt Crofters' Trust was not, in fact, the first example of crofting lands being held for the benefit of the crofting tenants, although it was the first where the legal owners of the croft lands were also the beneficial owners of those lands - the crofting tenants.

When Lord Leverhulme finally abandoned his plans to develop the Isle of Lewis[1] he offered, as a gift to the crofters, the title to their lands and to the people of Lewis various other properties including Lews Castle, the gas Company, the fish offal Company and the steam laundry, and all the farms and sporting and fishing rights in the parishes of Stornoway, Barvas, Uig and Lochs. Few crofters took up the offer of the crofts largely due to the fact that a crofter who owned his croft would be required to pay owner's rates as well as occupier's rates although there were other factors;[2] but the Town Council of Stornoway did accept the offer and so the town of Stornoway, its surrounding areas, Back/Tolsta and the Eye Peninsula were transferred into the ownership of the Stornoway Trust by a deed dated 12th November 1923. Of the 70,000 acres now administered by the Trust, some 65,000 acres are croft land comprising 45 townships and 1,347 crofts. The average croft size is between 3 and 4 acres. The estate is administered by 10 trustees who are elected by persons resident within the boundaries of the estate and who are entitled to vote at local government elections, an electorate which comprises some 10,219 people, roughly half of the total electorate of the Western Isles. The Stornoway Trust is not, therefore, to be regarded as just a crofting estate; many of the persons entitled to vote on elections of the trustees are not crofters. There is a full time estate factor and, currently, three full time members of staff. The main source of income of the Trust is mineral royalties, investment dividends, rents/leases (although crofting rents account for only a very small portion), capital receipts and wayleaves and it has charitable status. The trustees make the community and public interest their priority.[3]

Glendale in the North East of Skye is sometimes referred to as an example of crofting community ownership through a Trust and, indeed, of the pitfalls associated with such ownership, but this is, in fact, a misdescription. The Glendale estate was purchased in 1903 by the Congested Districts Board under the provisions of the Congested Districts (Scotland) Act 1897. The estate, which was purchased for £15,000, comprised some 20,000 acres of which a half was in the possession of the crofters and the remainder was land on which a flock of black faced sheep grazed. But the land was not to be held in trust for the crofters. Each of the crofting tenants was offered the right to buy his croft, the purchase price to be paid by an annuity, and a share in the black face sheep grazing farm to be operated as a club farm. One hundred and thirty-one crofters became owner occupiers.[4] The community aspect of the scheme involved the share in the club farm, but over the years the community aspect has diminished, particularly as a result of the sale of croft houses to incomers, and Glendale is now held up as an example of a community framework which did not work.[5] But Glendale is not an example of community ownership through a crofting Trust.

The idea of community ownership of croft lands through a crofting Trust had been mooted in the early 1970s by a working party set up by the Scottish Council of the Labour Party. The working party, set up to consider crofting policy, was strongly in favour of community ownership to be achieved by transferring all croft lands to an elected crofting Trust[6]. The Public Accounts Committee also recommended that the Scottish Office should dispose of all its crofting estates. But the proposals did not find favour with the Government of the day and it was not until 1989 that the idea of such a disposal was to resurface at the Scottish Crofters Union conference in that year. In February 1990 the Department of Agriculture and Fisheries for Scotland (DAFS) issued a Consultation Paper on the possible disposal of the DAFS' crofting estates to community ownership, making special reference to Skye and Raasay.[7] The Consultation Paper said that the idea of Trust ownership was not a new one, referring to the example of the Stornoway Trust and to the proposals, during the 1960s, by the Crofters Commission that common grazing lands should be vested in a Trust.[8] The Highlands and Islands Development Board and the Scottish Crofters Union asked the Arkleton Trust (Research) Limited to submit a report on the legal and practical implications of a transfer of the Skye and Raasay estates to community ownership. It was, of course, the report from the Arkleton Trust which formed the basis of the plans of the Assynt crofters for the formation of the Assynt Crofters' Trust. In the event, nothing came of the Government's proposals. There was no appetite amongst crofters on the DAFS' estates for community ownership. "Consultations indicated that the overwhelming majority of those affected preferred retention of the status quo. In the light of these views, and taking into account the practical and financial aspects, we have decided not to pursue the crofting

Trust concept further at this stage."[9]

But one of the questions asked in the Government's Consultation Paper was whether the approach being considered by the Secretary of State should also be considered by other crofting landlords. The Arkleton Trust report considered this question and suggested that it was, perhaps, premature to recommend this wider option for private estates when the procedures had not yet been applied to the DAFS' crofting estates. The report made the point that the purpose for which the Government had acquired those estates, to facilitate land settlement in the years following the First World War, was "... not necessarily the same as that which has motivated the acquisition of crofting estates by private landlords."[10] Indeed not. The report went on: "Should the possibilities of disposal of such [privately held] estates be considered by some landlords in the near future then the option of transfer to community ownership may be on the agenda. But, should a landlord wish to maximise the return from such a sale, it seems unlikely that this would be achieved by the transfer of ownership to a crofters' Trust - unless a source of funds could be found that, so far, remains undetected."[11] These words highlight the special circumstances which existed in Assynt in 1992. In the normal course, it would not have been expected that a privately held crofting estate would be available for purchase by the crofting tenants. But the liquidation of the corporate owner of the North Lochinver Estate and the threatened fragmentation of the estate broke the mould and the public interest generated in the purchase contributed to funds becoming available from these undetected sources.

We have seen, in earlier Chapters, how it was thought that the success of the Assynt Crofters' Trust might herald a new era in crofting land ownership. There has, however, been no headlong rush by crofters to form crofting Trusts to bid for their croft lands. In each of the cases which have followed Assynt there could be said to be special circumstances which encouraged, or contributed to, the purchase. In 1993, the crofters of Borve and Annishadder in Skye formed the Borve and Annishadder Township Trust, a Company limited by guarantee, which purchased the 4,596 acres of croft lands from the private landlord, Major J.A. MacDonald whose grandfather had tenanted Borve and Annishadder with crofters some 90 years before.[12] In this case the crofters had wanted to purchase hill land to plant trees for shelter and to make sheep gathering easier. The possibility of grant aid was a further incentive. While the landlord did not want to sell just that part of the estate, he was prepared to sell the whole estate because he had taken the view that crofting laws had made the running of such an estate difficult. He also considered that the crofters should have the responsibility for the land as owners. In discussions with the crofters, MacDonald suggested the possibility of a joint venture between the estate and the common grazings committee, but the crofters were not happy with this arrangement. And so the offer to sell the whole estate was made. Compared to Assynt, the capital required to purchase the estate was very small (some £20,000) and financial help was received from Skye and Lochalsh Enterprise (£5,000) and the Highland Fund provided a soft loan of £8,000. The main sources of income from the estate are croft rents and wayleaves from hydro poles. The estate has no salmon rivers or deer forests, but the Trust is looking at crofter forestry schemes and possible 'spin offs' from this, tourism and a possible wind generated electricity project and the Trust is also looking at community schemes for generating electricity from renewable resources. A pony trekking business has been set up.

The purchase on 4th April 1995, of the Island of Eigg by the Isle of Eigg Heritage Trust did not technically follow the Assynt model, but it certainly drew on the success of the Assynt crofters and the experience gained by them, particularly in relation to fund raising and publicity. It was the first time that a community had joined forces in partnership with local government (Highland Council) and a conservation body, Scottish Wildlife Trust.[13] In Assynt, the possibility of such a partnership had been considered and rejected.

Borve and Annishadder was followed in April 1996 by the transfer of the 10,770 acre Melness crofting estate in Sutherland[14] to Melness Crofters' Estate Limited. The estate comprised six townships and this transfer, again, was in special circumstances, involving as it did the free transfer of the estate by the owner, Michael Foljambe, as a way of securing the long term future of the estate. Indeed, Mr Foljambe, whose family had owned the estate since 1952, had first suggested the possibility of the crofters taking management responsibility for the croft lands some eight years before the transfer. The landowner revealed a refreshing view of the responsibilities of Highland crofting estate owners: "... I believe that crofters have the right to make their own decisions and apply for their own assistance from Enterprise Companies. Neither finance nor politics come into this decision and neither does class warfare. I just want the young people to be able to stay in the area."[15] Mr Foljambe was also motivated by his feeling of frustration that he could do nothing to help the community on his infrequent visits and by his belief that the crofters might be motivated to help themselves if they had ultimate responsibility for the land. Mr Foljambe described his gift as being an interesting experiment in social engineering.[16]

Melness has been followed by the transfer, at the end of

February 1999, of the Bhaltos crofting estate in the Uig area
of Lewis, the first crofting estate in the Western Isles to come
under community ownership since the foundation of the
Stornoway Trust. The estate, the scene of land raids in the
1920s, and which is all virtually under crofting tenure, has
some 70 crofting tenants and the crofters were offered the
first option to buy by the owner, James Gilchrist who also
made a private contribution which significantly reduced the
price for the estate.[17]

Michael Foljambe's reference to assistance from
Enterprise Companies reminds us, of course, of the
important part played by Highland and Islands Enterprise in
the Assynt bid, and on 12th June, 1997, HIE was asked by
the Minister of State, Brian Wilson, to set up a support unit
dedicated solely to community land initiatives. The aim of
the HIE Community Land Unit is to increase the role of
communities in the ownership and management of land
and land assets and the sustainable management of these
resources for the benefit of the community. Its objectives are
to promote, and provide advice and support for, community
led land purchases or management initiatives and to
contribute to research and development policies related to
community land initiatives. The Community Land Unit was
further strengthened in June 1998 by the establishment of a
Community Land Purchase Fund with an initial £250,000 to
be used to offer loans and to help HIE led acquisitions. Even
more recent support was announced in September 1998 by
the Government in the form of funds for land acquisitions to
be financed through the National Lottery.

At the end of October 1997, the Orbost estate in Skye was
purchased for the community by HIE/Skye and Lochalsh
Enterprise, the first major venture of the Community Land
Unit, with the intention of creating a new rural settlement
based on a mix of housing, smallholdings and business

workplaces, and with the long term aim of handing over title to a community based Trust. Orbost is not, of course, an example of a crofting Trust of the Assynt type, but it shows how the initiative in Assynt to take land into community ownership has been developed and taken forward.

At the beginning of March, 1999, the 17,000 acres of the Knoydart estate finally, after a considerable period of uncertainty, came into community ownership. Although not a crofting Trust, the purchase of the Knoydart estate for the community is a further development of community ownership in the Highlands.

• Recent Government moves towards crofting Trusts, and the idea of a Pan Highlands and Islands Crofting Trust •

In October 1995 Michael Forsyth, the then Secretary of State for Scotland, gave a further boost to the idea of the transfer of crofting estates, both privately and publicly owned, and it was the Assynt Crofters' Trust which he used as his blueprint. He issued a press announcement as to his proposals on 20th October, met with the Crofters Commission in Inverness and on the same day flew into Assynt for a meeting in Stoer community hall with representatives of the Assynt Crofters' Trust. He asked them, "What I want to know is whether you have found ownership has made a real difference, and if it has, can we do what you did ten times over?"[18] In his press announcement he said: "I am keen to encourage all crofters and crofting landlords to consider the crofting Trust option and as Secretary of State I am interested in transferring ownership of the substantial crofting lands I hold to crofting or community Trusts if there is sufficient interest and support at local level."

In December 1995 a Crofting Land Trust Steering Group (CLTG) comprising representatives of the Scottish Crofters Union, Comhairle nan Eilean and the Highland Council, with representatives of the Crofters Commission as observers, was formed and in January 1996 the CLTG decided, in principle, to set up a Pan Highlands and Islands Crofting Trust with the following objects:

- to encourage community ownership of land in the Highlands and Islands
- to increase the number of crofts and smallholdings
- to foster self-determination in crofting communities and community responsibility for land in their locality
- to act as heritable proprietors and landlords of such land
- to act as managers for other heritable proprietors and landlords of such land
- to manage lands for the benefit of the communities in the locality of such lands
- to apply all profits earned by the company to these objects.[19]

The Scottish Office Consultation Paper on the disposal of the Secretary of State's crofting estates was published in February 1996 and, in the foreword, Michael Forsyth said: "The recently established crofting Trusts at Assynt and Borve and Annishadder, and the long established Stornoway Trust, offer examples of how local communities can take effective control of their own affairs and I would like to see my current tenants having the same opportunities." The Paper referred to the idea of a Pan Highlands and Islands Crofting Trust and asked for views on such a Trust. The CLTG commissioned a study to assess the feasibility of establishing such a Trust, with particular reference to responding to the

Consultation Paper which posed the question of whether the Secretary of State's crofting estates "... would not be better run in the future by the local communities themselves."

The responses to the Scottish Office Consultation Paper showed[20] that while most of the respondents were broadly supportive of the Secretary of State's proposals for crofting Trusts and that while there was some interest in the idea of establishing Trusts, most of the respondents saw the status quo as the preferred option, and this, when taken with the fact that no responses were received from the majority of the Secretary of State's crofting estates, would suggest that there had been no real change in the views of crofters on these estates over the last six years or so. But some concern had been expressed during the consultations conducted for the Crofting Land Trust feasibility study as to whether the status quo was, in fact, a real alternative. There was a worry that financial circumstances might mean that the current deficit on these estates would have to be cut with consequent ramifications for quality of service and maintenance. Furthermore, an independent survey conducted by the Scottish Crofters Union during the autumn of 1995 showed that, overall, there was a low level of awareness of land tenure issues among crofters.[21]

As to the Pan Highlands and Islands Crofting Trust, the feasibility study concluded that it should be possible for such a Trust to assume responsibility for the ownership and management of the Secretary of State's crofting estates and to at least break even by about the fifth year of operation, assuming certain conditions were fulfilled - one of which was that all sporting and mineral rights should be transferred at no cost. The Trust, would be a Company limited by guarantee with the crofters of the estates owned by the Trust eligible as ordinary members and with associate non-voting membership open to other crofters and interested organisations. The feasibility study concluded that a Pan Highland

and Islands Crofting Trust would encourage crofting communities to become more interested in sustaining the practical value of the land for the community; would act as a stepping stone to local ownership (communities might, in time, wish to assume ownership and responsibility through their own Trust); would offer protection against possible future changes in the management of the Secretary of State's crofting estates (protecting against the perceived dangers of the status quo); would offer a safety net for local Trusts which might run into management difficulties (the problem that, over time, local Trusts might find it difficult to provide the required amount of management time for running the estate from local sources); would create local employment and a source of central services, expertise and information; and would allow for a vehicle to be created to raise funds towards future purchases of privately owned croft lands.[22]

On 20th October 1996, the Government introduced in the House of Lords a Bill to enable the Secretary of State to dispose of his crofting lands and certain other properties of his in the crofting counties to approved bodies and for connected purposes, and the Bill completed its final stages on 18th March 1997, passing into law as the Transfer of Crofting Estates (Scotland) Act 1997 (the 1997 Act), one of the final pieces of legislation of the Conservative Government. We turn now to consider the critical provisions of the 1997 Act relating to the assets to be transferred and the body or bodies to which such transfer may be made.[23]

Section 1 permits the Secretary of State to dispose of any of his crofting property on such terms as he, with the consent of the Treasury, may agree with the body acquiring the property and permits (but does not require) the disposal to include the mineral and sporting rights. It appears from the Parliamentary Debates that it was the intention of the Government that the vast majority of land would benefit from free transfer, particularly where a free transfer was necessary to ensure the viability of a Trust.[24] However the Earl of Lindsay gave an example of some estates consisting of individual crofts without any common grazings, largely to be found in the Eastern Highlands, where the land is very much better quality than the norm, where it was unlikely that a free transfer would be necessary to ensure economic viability.[25] But it was the issue of the transfer of mineral and sporting rights which was the subject of the closest examination. In his evidence given to the Scottish Select Committee, the factor of the Stornoway Trust said that the Trust's ownership of the mineral rights had been vital. The ability of the Trust to open a quarry and obtain royalties had been "... the turning of a corner" so far as the financial viability of the Trust had been concerned.[26] It will be recalled that one of the pre-conditions for the viability of a Pan Highlands and Islands Crofting Trust was that such rights should be transferred at no cost. It was clearly understood by the Government spokesmen that the transfer of these rights could make a vital contribution to the viability of a crofting Trust, but the debate centred on two concerns: on the permissive wording of the section - that the transfer may include the disposal of mineral and sporting rights, the Secretary of State was under no obligation; and on the fact that a transfer of these rights might be for significant sums of money. Behind the debate was the troubling echo of the treatment of mineral and sporting rights in relation to croft lands in crofting legislation ever since 1886.[27] A number of powerful attacks on these points were made. In the House of Lords, Lord Sewel, referring to the possibility that land would be transferred and the mineral and sporting rights retained, said : "Quite frankly, such a situation would be unacceptable. In many cases the mineral and sporting rights represent the only actual and potential route to economic viability; as importantly, the lack of such rights would seriously constrain the potential for future local development."[28] In the House of Commons, Mr McFall, referring to mineral and sporting rights said: "It is considered that those rights offer many crofts the only potential route to profitability. Without the transfer of those rights, the transfer of many crofts would not be viable. I am aware that the Government want flexibility in that regard, but reassurance is required by the crofters, and we want to be given it in the Bill."[29] In response to this, the Scottish Office Minister, Raymond Robertson, stated that, because sporting rights run with the land, sporting rights would be transferred automatically[30] and that the presumption was that mineral rights would, where possible, be included in the transfer but after a valuation and on payment of an appropriate charge. "If a prospective Trust is not initially able or willing to assume the relevant mineral rights, we propose that it should be able to benefit from the income while the Scottish Office retains the mineral rights ... Whatsoever arrangements are agreed must be fair to the Trust and the public purse, from where the money to acquire the estates and support them over the past decades came."[31] In light of this assurance the Opposition requests for an amendment were withdrawn.

Section 2 of the 1997 Act requires the Secretary of State only to dispose of his crofting estates to a body which he, after consultation with the Crofters Commission, considers to be representative of the crofting interests in the property to be disposed of and has as its primary objective the promotion of the interests of persons residing on that property. There is no specific mention of a crofting Trust, nor is there any specific reference to a Pan Highland Trust. However Mr Robertson explained that the intention was that transfer to a Pan Highlands and Islands Trust should be possible, but that, "the primary purpose of our initiative is to give ownership and control of the crofting estates to the crofters who live on them, and we would have to be satisfied that any Pan Highlands and Islands Trust achieved that objective. We would not be interested in a Pan Highlands and Islands Trust if it meant imposing a remote bureaucracy on reluctant crofters."[32] The words in section 2(1)(b) 'the promotion of the interests of persons residing on such property as its primary objective' are important. They require the Secretary of State, after consultation with the Crofters Commission, to be satisfied that the body which is to take the transfer should look after the interests of all the persons who reside on the estate - crofting and non-crofting alike.[33] Furthermore, the Government made it clear, in debate, that the Crofters Commission would, in consultation as to the appropriateness of the body to which the transfer was to be made, take account of local community development.[34]

There is no specific provision in the Act which places any restrictions on crofting Trusts from subsequently disposing of any of the assets transferred to it; no restrictions on Trusts making a 'quick buck' from such disposals,[35] a point which was pressed both at the Scottish Select Committee and, again, in debate in the Lords.[36] The Government, however, considered that there were sufficient existing protections in the planning laws and crofting law as to the removal of land from crofting tenure. Furthermore, to have such a restriction would place such a Trust in a different position from a crofting Trust of a private estate.[37]

• Crofting and Land Reform •

The ownership and management of croft lands is, of course, only part of the debate on land ownership and the case for land reform in Scotland. Over the last few years, the question 'who owns Scotland'? has been posed in a number of publications[38] but incredible as it may seem, there still exists a lack of readily available information about the ownership of land in Scotland. As this account has shown, the issue of land ownership in Scotland, particularly in the Highlands and Islands, still generates an enormous amount of passion, interest and strongly held views. In particular, the fact that the majority of the land consists of under 1,500 private estates, that much of Scotland's land is in foreign ownership, the prevalence of absentee landlordism, the increase in ownership by environmental non-Governmental organisations such as the National Trust for Scotland, the RSPB and the John Muir Trust,[39] all serve to keep the land issue firmly in the public consciousness. In October 1997 the Land Reform Policy Group was formed by the Government "to identify and assess proposals for land reform in rural Scotland, taking account of their cost, legislative and administrative implications and their likely impact on the social and economic development of rural communities and on the natural heritage." The Group published in February 1998, a discussion paper entitled, 'Identifying the Problems'. So far as crofting was concerned, the Group posed a number of questions as to the future for crofting and, in terms of community ownership, asked the question: "... would it make sense to look at ways to bring all other [i.e. privately held] crofting communities into a single simplified procedure for acquiring community ownership?"[40] In September 1998, the Group published a further paper entitled, 'Identifying the Solutions' which gave, in light of the contributions received on the first paper, its vision for the future. For crofting, the vision was for more sustainable crofting communities to be achieved by, amongst other steps, the right given to all crofting communities to take control of the land and by encouraging more community management of croft land.[41] The responses to the Group's first and second papers indicated that it was doubtful whether many communities would, in fact, exercise any right given to them to bring land into community ownership,[42] but though legislation was unlikely to be used, the Group considered that all crofting communities should be given a right to form a Trust and take control of their croft land similar to the right given by the 1997 Act in respect of the Secretary of State's crofting estates. The Group accepted that legislation on this would be controversial and drew attention to the possible difficulties under the European Convention on Human Rights, but considered that such legislation would act as a deterrent to unreasonable behaviour by landowners.[43] The Land Reform Policy Group published its final paper 'Recommendations for Action' in January 1999. So far as crofting Trusts were concerned, the Group recommended that there should be legislation which gave all crofting communities which create a properly constituted crofting Trust a right to have ownership of their croft land transferred to the Trust on fair financial terms. While the Group did not give further specific detail, it said that the legislation would aim to give all the other crofting communities the same basic rights to acquire their croft land as are given to the Secretary of State's croft tenants under the 1997 Act. The Group did, however, say that the legislation would need to deal with the mineral and sporting rights and the position of sporting tenants.[44] Behind that simple statement lies a considerable amount of debate to come and many of the issues raised in this book will be relevant to that debate.

• A vision for the future? •

The structure is now in place for the publicly owned crofting estates to be transferred to community ownership and there is the prospect of future legislation to facilitate the transfer of privately held estates to crofting Trusts.[45] Furthermore, through the Crofting Trusts Advisory Service, a partnership created by representatives from the Assynt Crofters' Trust, Borve Crofters, the Crofters Commission and the Highlands and Islands Enterprise, there exists the means by which crofters who are considering community ownership can be given independent information and advice.[46] And the Highlands and Islands Community Land Unit can provide important financial and other support. There is clearly enthusiasm, and the necessary technical and financial support, for more community owned land in the Highlands and Islands. But the extent to which the specific example of crofting Trusts in Assynt, Borve and Annishadder, Melness and Bhaltos, will have further followers will depend largely on the individual circumstances which exist in each crofting estate and in the townships, on the relationship the crofters have with their landlord, on the hopes and aspirations of the crofters in those townships and, perhaps most importantly, on the leadership which comes from individuals in the townships and the willingness of those people to devote the time and take on the responsibilities which go with managing a Trust and the estate and on the availability of assistance, through funding, which such people can be given. In Assynt, as we have seen, the principal pre-conditions for a crofter Trust bid were present; an unhappy crofter/landlord relationship, strong belief and strong leadership, and there was the further important dimension of a threatened fragmentation of the croft lands. To what extent, however, will this apply elsewhere across the crofting counties?

For those who do follow, there are a host of difficult issues which will have to be considered, issues which are not solved simply by giving communities the right to buy. The issue of conflicts of interest and tensions which was raised in Chapter

3 will be relevant but with the likely added dimension of the interests of the non-crofting community. In the case of Assynt, the land on the estate was, as we know, almost all croft land.[47] This will not necessarily be the case with other communities and the extent of the involvement of the non-crofting community in the Trust will need to be considered carefully. Where a crofting Trust does not involve almost wholly croft lands, there will certainly be people who live and work on the land but who are not crofters. They are still part of the community.[48] Exclusion of such people could, in time, lead to its own tensions. If community involvement means what it says, there is a clear case for their inclusion.[49] In the case of the transfer of the Secretary of State's crofting lands, of course, the 1997 Act requires the interests of the non-crofting community to be considered and for the primary objectives of the Trust to take account of croft and non-croft interests alike.

There are, undoubtedly, imperfections in the concept of the crofting Trust[50]. The extent of non-crofting community involvement, the issue of protecting the assets of the Trust for the community on a long term basis, the conflicts of interest and tensions, the difficulties of keeping up the momentum of community involvement and the pure economics of maintaining the crofting estate as a viable entity. Furthermore, while future legislation may secure the right for crofting communities to purchase their croft lands on fair financial terms (and that expression hides a fundamental divide between expectations of landlords and expectations of crofters) and while some public funding towards the purchase price will be available, there will still be difficulties in financing purchases. As John MacKenzie says: "Communities cannot appeal ad infinitum to the sympathy for the underdog and a sense of national conscience about what happened 200 years ago."[51] There

are also issues of wider interest concerning the encouragement of more community management of croft land, the
simplification of crofting legislation and administration
and the possibility of more local involvement in, and
accountability for, crofting administration. There is, as we
have seen, a serious burden placed by community buy-outs
on the available volunteer energy to manage the estate and
lack of funding available for local people to be paid to take
on such roles as a development officer. In a memorandum to
the Scottish Select Committee on the 1997 Act, John
MacKenzie made the point that for local management
responsibility inherent in a community buy-out to be
successful, there had to be recognition of the fact that
ongoing support for local management would be necessary.
He considered that insufficient attention was given to this in
the draft Bill being considered by the Committee and, in the
event, the 1997 Act was silent on the point.[52] All these are
important matters which will require serious and careful
consideration.

But the debate about these specific issues, important as,
no doubt it will be, and the fact that, so far as crofting estates
are concerned, the 'dominoes have not yet fallen', that there
has not been a 'wave of replica purchases', should not
obscure or detract from the underlying significance or
importance of the events of Assynt in 1993/4. There can be
little doubt that the success of the Assynt Crofters' Trust in
purchasing the North Lochinver Estate is to be measured,
not by reference to how many crofting communities take the
specific Assynt route, but in the way it broke the mould and
encouraged a sea change in attitudes. A number of people
had been proposing community land initiatives for some
time, making the case for crofters taking control of their own
destinies, in particular that crofters were perfectly able to
take charge of crofting themselves,[53] but it was the Assynt

bid which made people realise that such initiatives were more than barren theory or idle hopes. They could be made to work in practice. The success of the Assynt crofters caused, or at the very least contributed heavily to, a fundamental change in, and encouraged the open articulation of, the underlying thoughts and feelings of crofters and gave an insight into the possibilities open to crofters to take responsibility for their own destinies. In securing the croftlands of the North Lochinver Estate for the benefit of the community, the Assynt Crofters' Trust sought to challenge the past, to change generations of commercial landlordism into community landlordism, to throw off generations of inferiorisation and to present a vision for the future.

This account started with a historical introduction and it is fitting to end it by looking again into the past where, notwithstanding the trials of the time, the vision for the future could be seen.

First, we turn to the more recent writings of Norman MacCaig. In his poem 'A man in Assynt', he spoke, as we saw earlier, movingly of the agonies that commercial landlordism had brought to the Highlands and Islands. But he ended his poem with hope, a hope which the Assynt crofters helped to realise:

> *... And the mind*
> *behind the eye, within the passion,*
> *remembers with certainty that the tide will return*
> *and thinks, with hope, that that other ebb,*
> *that sad withdrawal of people, may, too,*
> *reverse itself and flood*
> *the bays and the sheltered glens*
> *with new generations replenishing the land*
> *with its richest of riches and coming, at last,*
> *into their own again.*[54]

Going further back into history, we are reminded that the oral tradition in the Gaidhealtachd is important in any story about the emotions and feelings of the Highlanders, and that, in relation to the land issue, the Gaelic songs and poems of the clearances and Crofters' War years are a vital record of those emotions and feelings. The motivation of the poets was the preservation of the traditional Gaelic community[55] and the development of commercial landlordism was antipathetic to traditional values.[56] This is shown, in particular, in the poetry of John Smith of Lewis. In his poem 'Spiorad a' Charthannais' (Sprint of Kindliness), Smith identified the cement of the community as kindliness, and the economic determinism that was prevalent in commercial landlordism "... was, in his opinion, at variance with the preservation of society based on mutual support."[57] It was, as we have seen, the development of commercial landlordism and this economic determinism which contributed so heavily to the break-up of the Highland way of life, of traditional values. But as Donald Meek says in the introduction to his anthology of the Gaelic poetry and songs of the 1800s: "A vision for the future was urgently needed. The real challenge for the successors of the militant crofters of the 1880s appears only in the final verse of [an anonymous poem written in Skye in 1887] which anticipates further struggle for ownership of the land, as the battle had not yet ended:

> *'S on fhuair sinn nis ceann-feadhna,*
> *Cha stad sinn latha no oidhche,*
> *Gus am buannaich sinn an oighreachd*
> *Gu h-aoibhneach 's gu h-urramach.*

(And since we have now found a leader,
we will not cease by day or night
until we win possession of the estate
joyfully and honourably.)"[58]

These words might be said to be prophetic of what was to happen in Assynt in 1993. Certainly possession of the North Lochinver Estate was won and won joyfully and honourably. The crofters had a vision, not just to occupy the lands as tenants, not just to buy their own crofts, but to take managerial control over the estate and, thus, their own future, to take responsibility for the development of their land for the benefit of the community. In a strange twist, then, the commercial potential of land, which had contributed so much to the violation of *dùthchas* and to the clearances, which had caused the destruction of communities was now something the crofters could use for the benefit of their own community. Indeed, one author believes that the success of the Assynt crofters signifies the re-establishment of *dùthchas*.[59] Commercial landlordism forced many people off the land. The Highlanders fought for, and won, the right never to be evicted again. They also won the right to own their own individual crofts. What the Assynt Crofters' Trust did in 1993 was to take the development of the crofting community a stage further. Just as the commercial use of land caused such hardship in the past, might it not be that through vehicles such as the Assynt Crofters' Trust, it could be developed by crofters for the benefit of the community in the future? Not commercial landlordism, but community landlordism. Economic determinism, perhaps, but now qualified heavily by community interest, community values; the interaction of economic and social determinism. Might this not be the vision for the future which the anonymous poet was looking to?

Notes

1 For a discussion of Lord Leverhulme's proprietorship of Lewis, the reader is referred to Nicolson, N, *Lord of the Isles; Lord Leverhulme in the Hebrides,* London, 1960, Leneman, Leah, *Fit For Heroes?* Aberdeen, 1989, pp. 118-25 and Hunter, James, *The Making of the Crofting Community,* Edinburgh, 1976, pp. 197-206

2 See Nicolson, N, *Lord of the Isles; Lord Leverhulme in the Hebrides,* London, 1960, pp. 200 & 201 and *The Stornoway Gazette,* 4th October, 1923

3 Source: *The Crofter,* March, 1996 (Special Edition) and *SSC Evidence.* See also, Thompson, Frank, Land in Community Ownership - Sixty years of the Stornoway Trust, in Hulbert, J., (Ed), *Land: Ownership and Use,* Andrew Fletcher Society, 1986, and the *Stornoway Gazette* of 25th February, 1999 for an edited extract of a speech by James Shaw Grant at the 75th anniversary dinner of the Stornoway Trust

4 Cameron, E. A., *Land for the People? The British Government and the Scottish Highlands, c. 1880-1925,* East Lothian, 1996, p. 97

5 Wightman, Andy, *Who Owns Scotland?* Edinburgh, 1996, p. 181 (see also p. 58 and 150 above). See also McHattie, Angus, Crofting - Is there a Future? in Hulbert J., (Ed), *Land:Ownership and Use,* Andrew Fletcher Society, 1986, p.48. Glendale is also an example of the difficulties which can be encountered in getting agreement from a large group of crofters on matters of common interest. Speaking on the Grampian Television programme broadcast on 13th December 1993, a Glendale crofter referred to the difficulties of getting 147 people to agree on anything. He also spoke of the problems caused by crofters selling their houses to meet the demands of incomers and 'white settlers'.

6 Hunter, James, *The Claim of Crofting,* Edinburgh, 1991, p. 141

7 See Hunter, J., The DAFS Crofting Estates - A Case for Community Control, in Hulbert, J., (Ed), *Land:Ownership and Use,* Andrew Fletcher Society, 1986

8 This was, of course, part of the Commission's proposals that all crofts should pass into owner occupation (see Hunter, James, *The Claim of Crofting,* Edinburgh, 1991, Chapter 5)

9 Lord Strathclyde, Minister of State at the Scottish Office. For a summary of the responses to the Consultation Paper, see *West Highland Free Press* 27th October, 1995, p. 7

10 *Arkleton Trust Report,* para. 4.3

11 *Arkleton Trust Report,* para 4.3

12 For a commentary on the purchase, see Edinburgh University, *Access to the Land - A case study approach to Community Access to the Land Resource* by the Centre for Human Ecology University of Edinburgh, Ross and Cromarty District Council and others, March, 1996

13 Dressler, Camille, *Eigg-The Story of an Island,* Edinburgh, 1998, p. 186

14 For a description of Melness as a crofting community, see Coull, James, Melness - A crofting community on the North coast of Scotland, in *Scottish Studies,* vol 7, 1963, pp. 180-198

15 Quoted in *Am Bratach,* November, 1995, p. 3

16 Letter dated 10th April 1996 from Mr G.M.T. Foljambe to the Private Secretary to the Secretary of State for Scotland, being a response to the Consultation Paper, February, 1996

17 See *West Highland Free Press,* 20th November, 1998 and 5th March, 1999 and the *Stornoway Gazette,* 4th March, 1999

18 Quoted in *Am Bratach,* November, 1995, p. 3

19 Source: *Crofting Land Trust Feasibility Study,* para 1.1

20 Source: *Crofting Land Trust Feasibility Study,* para 2.5 and 2.6

21 See letter dated 29th April 1996 from the SCU to the Scottish Office Agriculture, Environment and Fisheries Department, being a response to the Consultation Paper, February, 1996

22 *Crofting Land Trust Feasibility Study,* para E5

23 The Parliamentary Debates on the Bill are to be found in *Hansard,* HL vol 575 cols 22, 870, 894, 1351; vol 577: cols CWH1, 1470; vol 578: col 121. HC vol 292: col 729. See also *SSC Evidence*

24 See, for example, *Hansard,* HL vol 577 col CWH4

25 *Hansard,* HL vol 577 col CWH4

26 *SSC Evidence,* para 92 and 96

27 See page 183 below. This was something to which Robert Maclennan and Brian Wilson drew attention in the debate on the Bill in the House of Commons; see *Hansard* HC vol 292, cols 731 and 732

28 *Hansard,* HL vol 575, col 876

29 *Hansard,* HC vol 292, col 731

30 But if sporting rights *are* transferred automatically why then does the legislation refer to the Secretary of State as still having a discretion over sporting rights? The point was also the subject of close questioning in the Scottish Select Committee - see *SSC Evidence,* para 10-14, 210-214 and page 59

31 *Hansard,* HC vol 292, col 733

32 *Hansard,* HC vol 292, col 745-746

33 *Hansard,* HL vol 577, col CWH12

34 *Hansard,* HL vol 577, col 1484

35 *SSC Evidence* para 146

36 *Hansard,* HL vol 577, col CWH14 and 1482

37 *Hansard,* HL vol 577, col CWH15

38 Notably, Wightman, Andy, *Who Owns Scotland?* Edinburgh, 1996, and Cramb, Auslan, *Who Owns Scotland Now? The use and abuse of private land,* Edinburgh and London, 1996, following John MacEwan's seminal work published in 1977 (McEwan, John, *Who Owns Scotland?* Edinburgh, 1977) and Callandar, Robin, *How Scotland is Owned,* Edinburgh, 1998

39 There have been separate calls for such organisations to join in a federation with other non-profit landowners such as crofting and community Trusts to counter the powers of the private landlords - see, for example, *The Scotsman,* 7th March, 1998. See also, Wightman, Andy, Not for Profit Landowning Organisations in the Highlands and Islands of Scotland, *Highlands and Islands Enterprise,* December, 1996, and Boyd, Graham, To Restore the Land to the People and the People to the Land, in *The Scottish Journal of Community Work and Development,* volume 3, Spring, 1998.

40 Land Reform Policy Group, *Identifying the Problems,* The Scottish Office, February, 1998 (hereafter *Identifying the Problems*) para 5.6

41 Land Reform Policy Group, *Identifying the Solutions,* The Scottish Office, September, 1998 (hereafter *Identifying the Solutions*) p. 104

42 Out of a total of 846 responses to *Identifying the Solutions,* only 46 responses came from individual crofters - see *Recommendations for Action,* p.24

43 *Identifying the Solutions*, p. 77 and p. 80

44 Land Reform Policy Group, *Recommendations for Action*, The Scottish Office, January, 1999 (hereafter *Recommendations for Action*) para 6.2

45 *Recommendations for Action*, para 6.2

46 The CTAS package includes the basic criteria and 80% funding for the necessary feasibility study and initial legal costs up to a maximum of £3,200 - see the *Crofting Trusts Advisory Service Explanatory Booklet*

47 However, even in Assynt some 20 per cent of the population on the estate are not crofters and are thus, for the present, excluded from membership of the Trust. The question as to whether these people should be allowed to become members of the Trust has been raised and, so far, rejected. It must, however, be a question for the future as to whether non-crofting community involvement in, and membership of, the Trust should be allowed.

48 And there will also be cases, like Orbost, where it may also be relevant to involve communities close to, but not part of, the estate. *West Highland Free Press*, 12th December, 1997

49 See, for example, *SSC Evidence*, para 150

50 The vehicle to be used - Company or Trust, each has its difficulties (see pages 56-60. Furthermore, a leading author has stated that while the principle of expanding community ownership through crofting Trusts remains sound, the crofting Trust fails to address certain fundamental issues. See Wightman, Andy, *Who Owns Scotland?* Edinburgh 1996, p. 180. James Hunter also argues that, for crofting to work better than it does, the whole structure of crofting administration needs to be addressed with the need to find a means of putting crofters in control of crofting - see Hunter, J., *Crofting Works - But it could and should work better*, Sabhal Mòr lecture, Skye, 1990. The problems (referred to on page 53 above) associated with the fact that each crofter retains the right to buy his croft and so take it out of the Trust need also to be addressed.

51 *Financial Times*, 9th January, 1999

52 *SSC Evidence*, page 20. It is interesting to note that the feasibility study and business plan drawn up for the Assynt Crofters' Trust made the point that the development of employment opportunities on the estate and the encouragement of individual crofters to undertake development schemes, would require the appointment of a temporary project officer funded from public agencies. The North West Development Programme has showed the value of such a project officer in providing the kind of stimulus required. In the event, no such financial help was forthcoming and John MaKenzie believes that the Trust has suffered because of the lack of development assistance.

53 In particular, James Hunter. See, e.g. Hunter, James, *The Claim of Crofting*, Edinburgh, 1991 and *The Crofter*, June, 1992, p. 6

54 MacCaig, Norman, *Collected Poems - A New Edition,* London, 1993, p.231

55 Meek, Donald E., *Tuath is Tighearna - Tenants and Landlords*, Edinburgh, 1995, p. 34. This motivation is still important. In discussing the future for land reform in Scotland, Robin Callandar said that proposals for land reform in Scotland should reflect "... community traditions and the legacies of indigenous Gaelic tenure." Callandar, Robin, *How Scotland is Owned,* Edinburgh, 1998, p. 170

56 Meek, Donald E., *Tuath is Tighearna - Tenants and Landlords*, Edinburgh,

1995, p. 35

57 Meek, Donald E., *Tuath is Tighearna - Tenants and Landlords,* Edinburgh, 1995, p. 35

58 Meek, Donald E., *Tuath is Tighearna - Tenants and Landlords,* Edinburgh, 1995, p. 40

59 Dressler, Camille, *Eigg - The Story of an Island,* Edinburgh, 1998, p. 174

APPENDIX

• The Legislative Background •

A croft is a small piece of land surrounded by a great deal of legislation giving rise to a lot of litigation

Crofting law is, without doubt, complex.[1] It is, however, important, for our story of the Assynt crofters, to have an appreciation of the importance of the rights which crofters have, and do not have, under the legislation.[2] In 1992/1993 the complex provisions of the legislation were to play an important part in the campaign of the Assynt Crofters' Trust, albeit not in their actual use but in the threat to use them, and albeit not in a way which the framers of the legislation might have foreseen. While the purchase in 1993 of the North Lochinver Estate did not, directly, involve the then current crofting legislation, the campaign by the Assynt Crofters' Trust did make significant psychological use of the rights available to crofters under the crofting legislation, in particular the right to buy. Furthermore, while crofters have significant rights under the legislation, there are also significant gaps in these rights, gaps which might be said to have hindered crofters from being able fully to exploit the potential of the land and benefit from opportunities for development[3] and it was an important part of the Assynt Crofters' Trust campaign that the Trust should obtain these missing rights and that they should be under 'sensitive local control' and used for the benefit of the community. So to put the campaign by the Assynt Crofters' Trust in a legislative context, this Appendix gives a brief introduction to certain features of the legislative framework. For a detailed consideration, the reader is referred to the various crofting law publications.[4]

The Crofters Holdings (Scotland) Act 1886 introduced a form of land tenure which was unique and it was founded on three principles: security of tenure, fair rent and compensation for tenants' improvements. It also gave a limited right for a crofter to bequeath his croft to any one member of his close family. Between 1886 and 1955 further Acts of Parliament were passed to amend and add to the 1886 Act, but it was not until 1976, with the passing of the Crofting Reform (Scotland) Act 1976 that the claim of crofters to a status higher than that of just protected tenants was recognised. The 1976 Act gave to a crofter the right to buy his croft house and inbye (or croft) land and also the right to buy any part of the common grazing which was adjacent or contiguous to his croft and which had been apportioned to his croft for his exclusive use. In 1993 the Crofters (Scotland) Act was passed as a consolidating measure and so the right to buy provisions of the 1976 Act are now contained in the 1993 Consolidation Act.

Alongside the important rights briefly described above, the legislation also makes provision for financial assistance to be given to crofters in two ways. (There are, of course, a large number of other grant schemes available to crofters aimed at land use, including the basic support for livestock production available to all farmers, but the following schemes are directed specifically at crofting.) The first is by way of agricultural improvement grants for the purpose of aiding and developing agricultural production on crofts,[5] the current scheme for which is administered under the Crofting Counties Agricultural Grants (Scotland) Scheme 1988. The assistance available is for a wide variety of agricultural operations such as land improvement, drainage, reseeding and fencing and the provision of farm equipment and agricultural buildings. This assistance is available not only to crofters but also to those who have exercised their

right to buy the croft and inbye land, provided they are of
substantially the same economic status as crofters. In other
words, the income of an unmarried applicant must be less
than the average earnings of a single male worker in the
manufacturing industry (this means test is a striking
indication of the assumed earnings of a crofter) or, if the
applicant is married, the limit is raised to take account of half
the average earnings of a female worker in the manufacturing industry. The 'economic status' test is important and it
has influenced to a marked degree the extent to which the
right to buy provisions of the legislation have been utilised.
Applicants are required to give information about all their
taxable income, as well as that of their spouse, for the last
three years. Because it has been seen as a means test it has
acted as a brake on the free operation of these provisions.[6]

The second is by way of building grants and loans under
the Crofters Building Grants and Loans Scheme.[7] Under this
Scheme the Secretary of State provides assistance by way of
grant or loan or by the supply of building or other materials
towards the erection, improvement or rebuilding of dwelling
houses and other buildings for crofters or towards the
provision or improvement of roads, or water or electricity or
gas supplies for domestic use. In this case, the assistance is
only available to crofters but if a crofter has applied for, and
the Secretary of State has agreed to provide, the assistance
and then exercises his right to buy the croft, he is not dis-
qualified from receiving the assistance and crofters who
purchase their croft or croft house remain eligible for
assistance for a new house or for improving an existing
house for a period of up to seven years from the date of the
purchase. Owner occupiers of crofts without a croft house or
with only a derelict or ruined house are not eligible for
assistance.[8] The Secretary of State can also provide
assistance by way of loan to an incoming tenant of a croft to

enable him to pay the outgoing tenant or the landlord any compensation for permanent improvements due to the outgoing tenant.

We turn now to look briefly at the two specific features of the crofting legislation underlying the campaign by the Assynt Crofters' Trust to purchase the North Lochinver Estate: the right given to crofters by the 1976 Act to buy the croft land and croft house and the fact that, notwithstanding the very important rights crofters have in respect of their lands, the ability to benefit from opportunities to develop the land remains largely with the landlord, a feature which, as we shall see, also affects the right to buy provisions.

• The right to buy •

Before the 1976 Act it was, of course, possible for a crofter to buy his own croft and become an owner occupier if he could reach agreement with his landlord. What the 1976 Act did was to give to crofters the right to apply to the Land Court for an order requiring the landlord to sell the croft if the landlord and the crofter could not reach agreement. The 1976 Act meant that the crofters' tenancy could really be described as a form of property.[9]

Under the right to buy provisions now contained in the 1993 Consolidation Act,[10] the crofter has the right to buy his croft dwelling house and his inbye land. The right does not extend to the common grazing unless it has been apportioned to the croft under the legislation and it is adjacent or contiguous to the croft. There is also an exception for the arable machair lands typically found in the Outer Isles. Furthermore, and importantly, the right does not extend to mines, metals or minerals or to salmon fishings relating to the croft land or to the croft dwelling house,[11] and the shooting and fishing rights of the landlord over the croft land are protected because the Land Court can order the acquiring crofter to grant a sporting lease of the shooting or fishing rights to the landlord if the Land Court is satisfied that if it were not granted, the interests of the landlord in those shooting or fishing rights would be materially affected. The sporting lease would be for a period of not less than twenty years and be at a nominal rent. The right to be granted a sporting lease was examined in a case heard before the Land Court in 1977.[12] In this case the landlord had applied to the Land Court to be granted, on the sale of the croft, a lease of the fishing rights to protect his valuable salmon fishing rights. The Court referred to the fact that the crofter was acquiring croft land and that the definition of croft land clearly excluded the right to salmon fishings; so, as the landlord retained the right to the salmon fishings, there was no need to grant a lease of these rights. Nor was there any need to grant a lease of the trout fishing rights because the right to salmon fishing included the right to trout fishing. However, the Court also held that the right to trout fishing was not, as in the case of the salmon fishings, an exclusive right and so the landlord who retained the exclusive right to salmon fishing could not prevent the crofter who had acquired his croft (or anyone authorised by the crofter) from fishing for trout in these waters. The landlord was not, the Land Court held, entitled to be granted a lease, therefore, to give him the exclusive right to the trout fishings.

So, on the exercise of the right to buy provisions, the landlord's commercial interest in the land, so far as mines, metals and minerals and salmon fishing is concerned, is given complete protection but his trout fishing rights are not fully protected.

In the absence of an agreement between the crofter and the landlord as to the purchase price for the inbye land, there is a straightforward statutory formula - normally fifteen times the current rent of the land purchased.[13] In the absence of agreement of a price for the croft dwelling house, the legislation provides for the price to be the open market value of the bare site of the dwelling house and half the open market value of the site which is attributable to any of the landlord's fixed equipment on the site.[14]

The right to buy provisions have not been greatly used by crofters who have not, generally, considered it to be particularly advantageous to be owner occupiers. The most common purchase has been of the croft house site and garden ground. The level of owner occupation varies considerably between areas, generally increasing towards the east and ranging from hardly any in the Western Isles to over 75 per cent. in Orkney where the croft land is capable of significant agricultural improvement and where land in the ownership of the farmer rather than under a crofting lease can be used as security for capital raising for the improvements.[15] After the right to buy provisions have been exercised, the land remains subject to the controls of the crofting legislation but the crofting tenancy is extinguished and the new owner becomes the owner of a vacant croft and the protective provisions of the legislation cease to apply to him. The owner occupier can apply to the Land Court for a decrofting direction to release the land from the legislation. In the absence of such a direction the Crofters Commission could ask the owner occupier to re-let the croft to a suitably qualified person. However the Commission takes a practical view of the situation and, so long as the former crofter or a member of his family continues to occupy and work the croft and fulfil any township obligations, it is the policy of the Crofters Commission not to seek re-letting proposals.

The legislation also provides for the landlord to be given some interest in a future sale of all or part of the croft land (but not the dwelling house) by the owner occupier to anyone who is not a member of the owner's family, if that sale is within five years of the date of acquisition by the crofter. Under the 'clawback' provisions contained in the legislation[16] the crofter is required to pay to the landlord a sum equal to one half of the market value of the croft land at the date of the disposal (after deducting the sum paid by the crofter to the landlord on the original purchase). So, again, the landlord is entitled to the residual commercial value of the croft land or, in this case, a share in that value. However, as we saw in Chapter 2, the Whitbread case had a significant effect on these 'clawback' provisions and meant that the Assynt crofters could use the right to buy provisions of the legislation, nominate a landlord to, as it were, hold the title to the land on their behalf and remain as crofting tenants. But it will be seen from the above that purchase of the crofting lands of the North Lochinver Estate through the right to buy provisions in the legislation would not have given to the Assynt crofters the full rights in the land they were seeking.

• It is a lesson of history that anything worth having in the Highlands is owned by somebody else - usually the landlord •

The fundamental principle of crofting law is that the crofter has security of tenure. He is entitled not to be removed from his croft except:

- where one year's rent of the croft is unpaid
- where the removal is specifically allowed by legislation (for example where the land is resumed by the landlord
- for a 'reasonable purpose')
- where there is a breach of one of the 'statutory conditions'

These statutory conditions are important because they make it clear that the underlying rights in the land remain with the landlord. This is interesting, particularly in those cases where "the land has been from time immemorial possessed by the crofter and his forbears and where there is no evidence that the land has ever been in the natural possession of its owner."[17] The statutory conditions require the crofter to pay his rent, to cultivate his croft, not, to the prejudice of the landlord, to injure the croft by letting the buildings run down or the soil deteriorate. The crofter cannot, without the consent of the landlord, put a building on his croft land. The legislation reserves further important rights over the land to the landlord as part of the statutory conditions. They include:

- the right to mine and take minerals
- quarrying rights
- the use of spring water for the estate to the extent not needed by the croft
- the right to cut and take timber and peats (apart from peats required by the croft and timber planted by the crofter or his predecessor)
- the right to open and make roads, fences and drains
- the right to pass to and from the sea shore or any loch[18]
- the right of hunting, shooting, fishing or taking game or fish, wild birds or vermin.[19]

These are all important rights and, taken together, mean that the commercial use and development of the land is reserved to the landlord. Of course, to take advantage of them, the landlord might well have to terminate the tenancy of a croft. As we have seen, the legislation provides for the landlord to apply to the Land Court for an authorisation to resume[20] possession of the land for himself "for some reasonable purpose having relation to the good of the croft or of the estate or to the public interest."[21] If the Land Court authorises the resumption, the crofter is given compensation for the loss of his croft. This compensation may be given by the crofter getting a tenancy of land of equivalent value in the neighbourhood or by adjustment in the rent payable or by a money payment.[22] However the legislation also gives the right to the crofter to share in the development value of the land resumed and this further compensation includes a share in 'the value of the land resumed'.[23] But there is an important limitation on the extent of this compensation for development value. In a case heard before the Court of Session in 1993,[24] a small piece of grazing land at Oldshoremore in Sutherland was resumed by the landlord so that it could be let to the Highland Regional Council for gravel extraction. One might have assumed that the compensation paid to the crofter would include the value of the minerals. As counsel for the crofters had argued, the intention behind the legislation was surely that the crofters should be entitled to share in the development value of the land taken out of crofting use. Unfortunately the Court did not agree. It was held that the words 'the value of the land resumed' only covered the land which the landlord had, in fact, resumed. As we have seen in the statutory conditions, the mineral rights in croft lands are reserved to the landlord and so the landlord had not resumed them - he had never been parted from them. It therefore followed in the opinion of the Court of Session that the crofters were not entitled to a share in the value of the mineral rights. Commenting on the case, Donald MacLeod, the President of the Scottish Crofters Union, said, "It's a lesson of history that anything worth having in the Highlands is owned by somebody else - usually the landlord."[25] One is reminded of the words of Mary MacPherson (Màiri Mhòr nan Oran), the famous 19th century Gaelic poet from Skye in her poem, *Eilean a' Cheò*

(The Isle of the Mist) where she wrote of the wealth in the land and of the right of the Highlanders to it:

> *But remember that you are a people,*
> *and maintain your right -*
> *there is wealth beneath the mountains,*
> *where you were brought up;*
> *there are iron and coal there,*
> *and grey lead and gold,*
> *and there are mines for your profit*
> *in the green Isle of the Mist.*

But this wealth was not given to the crofters by the 1886 Act, or by the right to buy provisions of the 1976 Act. Nor, more recently, did the Transfer of Crofting Estates (Scotland) Act 1997 include a right to this wealth.[26]

Even where the legislation has been amended to help crofters share in the commercial development of croft land, it has not always been successful. In 1991, the Crofters Forestry (Scotland) Act 1991 was passed to enable crofters to use their land for 'forestry purposes'. However the legislation has been framed in such a way that it is doubtful whether crofters can proceed with a scheme to plant trees or to cut them down or sell the timber produced without the approval of the estate landlord. "It would come as a surprise to most crofters who had planted trees on their own land if they were to be prevented from felling them and, still worse, from disposing of them as their own."[27] The problem in relation to cutting and selling appears to have been solved by the formulation of a model agreement where these rights can be agreed, but the refusal of a landlord can be problematic because no reasons need be given and there is no right of appeal. In referring to the limited rights which crofters have to engage in developing their land to the Scottish Select

Committee on the Transfer of Crofting Estates (Scotland) Bill, a memorandum from the Scottish Crofters Union said: "... it is only five years ago that crofters gained the right to plant a tree although they as yet do not have the right to cut it down."[28] In practice there have been three formal refusals; one led to a buy-out of the land by the crofters, a second scheme eventually went ahead after the landlord was re-petitioned and the third is unresolved.[29] It seems, however, that crofters who want to use their land for commercial forestry would need to obtain a good deal more than just the consent of the landlord and the approval of the Crofters Commission. These problems have, however been recognised by the Land Reform Policy Group and the Group has proposed that there should be legislation to "... clarify the right of crofters to plant trees on their land and to give them a clear right to exploit the trees they plant for timber and other purposes including the right to sell the timber and timber products."[30]

Notes

1   A croft has been referred to as a small piece of land surrounded by a great deal of legislation giving rise to a lot of litigation

2   It should be noted that with the publication of two important papers, *Recommendations for Action* by the Land Reform Policy Group and *The Way Forward* by the Crofters Commission, crofting legislation is currently under intense scrutiny and, to some extent, in a state of flux. In addition to the Land Reform Policy Group's recommendations for legislation which have been discussed above, the Crofters Commission is to draw up action plans for the consideration of six principal issues concerning crofting: community empowerment, culture, employment, housing, land use and the environment and regulation. It remains to be seen what this will mean for the role of crofting in the rural community

3   Flyn, Derek and Graham, Keith, *Crofters (Scotland) Act 1993,* Edinburgh, 1994, p.3

4   MacCuish, Donald, and Flyn, Derek, *Crofting Law,* Edinburgh, 1990; Flyn, Derek and Graham, Keith, *Crofters (Scotland) Act 1993*, Edinburgh, 1994; *Guide to the Crofting Acts,* Crofters Commission, September 1997. See also Agnew, Sir Crispin, When is a croft not a croft? in *Journal of the Law Society of Scotland,* March, 1991

5   Section 42(1) *1993 Consolidation Act*

6   MacCuish, D. J., Crofting Legislation since 1886, in *Scottish Geographical Magazine,* vol 103, No 2, 1987, p. 93

7   Section 42(4)&(5) *1993 Consolidation Act*

8   *CBGLS Guidance Notes,* 1995, p. 8

9   Flyn, Derek and Graham, Keith, *Crofters (Scotland) Act 1993,* Edinburgh, 1994, p. 3

10   Sections 12 to 19 *1993 Consolidation Act*

11   Section 12(3) and (4) *1993 Consolidation Act*

12   Ferguson v. Ross Estates Co. Ltd [1977]SLT (Land Court) 19

13   Section 14 *1993 Consolidation Act*

14   Section 15 *1993 Consolidation Act*

15   Of the total number of registered crofts, at 31st March 1998 18.9% were known to be owner occupied. For Lewis the figure was 0.64%, for the Outer Isles, including Harris, Barra, North and South Uist, 2%, for Skye and the Small Isles, 15.4%, for Orkney was 75.9% and for Sutherland the figure was 18.2% (Source: *The Crofters Commission Annual Report for 1997/98)*

16   Section 14(3) *1993 Consolidation Act*

17   MacCuish, Donald J., and Flyn, Derek, *Crofting Law,* Edinburgh, 1990, p. 104

18   For an interesting example of the rights of landlords in a similar context and the effects such rights can have on the development of local resources by crofters, see *West Highland Free Press,* 14th March, 1997

19   Schedule 2 *1993 Consolidation Act*

20   'resume' is an interesting word given that in some cases there will be no evidence of the landlord ever having had possession of the land!

21   Section 20(1) *1993 Consolidation Act.* It should be noted that the Land Reform Policy Group has proposed, without giving further detail, that control over decrofting through resumption should be tightened by redefining 'reasonable purpose' - see *Recommendations for Action,*

para 6.2

22 Section 20(1) *1993 Consolidation Act*
23 Section 21 *1993 Consolidation Act*
24 MacKenzie v. Barr's Trustees [1993] *SLT* 1228
25 Quoted in *Northern Times* 4th June, 1993
26 See Chapter 5
27 Flyn, Derek and Graham, Keith, *Crofters (Scotland) Act 1993*, Edinburgh, 1994, p. 52
28 *SSC Evidence*, para 45
29 *Am Bratach* No 71, 1997, p. 15 ('A crofter's guide to forestry', by Chris Marsh)
30 *Recommendations for Action*, para 6.2

BIBLIOGRAPHY

1. Records and Official publications

Annual Reports of *The Crofters Commission*

Arkleton Trust Report on the Future of the DAFS Estates in Skye and
  Raasay, June, 1990

Assynt Crofters' Trust unpublished papers, newsletters and news
  updates

Consultation Paper on Possible Disposal of The Secretary of State
  for Scotland's Crofting Estates to Community Ownership,
  Department of Agriculture and Fisheries for Scotland, February,
  1990

Consultation Paper on The Disposal of The Secretary of State's
  Crofting Estates to Crofting Trusts, Scottish Office, Agriculture
  Environment and Fisheries Department, February, 1996
  and the Responses

Crofters' Etc Building Grants and Loans Scheme (CBGLS) - Guidance
  Notes published by the Scottish Office, February, 1995

Crofting Land Trust Feasibility Study - Final Report issued October,
  1996 by Independent Northern Consultants

Documents relating to the campaign by the Assynt Crofters' Trust
  1992-93 (National Library of Scotland) - (the Assynt Crofters'
  Trust Papers)

Guide to the Crofting Acts, *Crofters Commission*, September, 1996

Hansard Reports of Parliamentary Debates

Identifying the Problems, Land Reform Policy Group, The Scottish
  Office, February, 1998 and the Responses

Identifying the Solutions, Land Reform Policy Group, The Scottish
  Office, September, 1998 and the Responses
  Minutes of evidence of the Scottish Select Committee on the
  Transfer of Crofting Estates (Scotland) Bill, 12 December, 1996,
  HL Paper 27 (*SSC Evidence*)

Recommendations for Action, Land Reform Policy Group, The Scottish
  Office, January, 1999

Report of the Commissioners of Inquiry into the conditions of the
  Crofters and Cottars in the Highlands and Islands of Scotland
  (Napier Report) C-3980, 1884

The Way Forward - the Role of Crofting in Rural Communities,
  The Crofters Commission, 1998

2. Newspapers and periodicals

Am Bratach
Caithness Courier
Daily Telegraph
Guardian
Inverness Courier
Morning Star
Press & Journal
The Scotsman
Shetland Times
West Highland Free Press
The Crofter
Financial Times

Assynt News
Daily Record
The Herald
The Independent
The Northern Times
The Oban Times
Scenes
Scottish Farmer
Stornoway Gazette
You Magazine
The Sunday Times

3. Books, pamphlets and articles

Adam, R. .J., *Papers on Sutherland Estate Management*, Edinburgh, 1972

Agnew, Sir Crispin, When is a croft not a croft? *Journal of the Law Society of Scotland*, March, 1991, pp. 115-119

Bangor-Jones, Malcolm, The Establishment of Crofting in North West Sutherland, *Am Bratach*, June and July, 1993

Bangor-Jones, Malcolm, Assynt Resists, *Am Bratach*, Jan-March, 1995

Bangor-Jones, Malcolm, *The Assynt Clearances*, Dundee, 1998

Boyd, Graham, To Restore the Land to the People and the People to the Land - The emergence of the Not-for-Private-Profit Land Ownership Sector in the Highlands and Islands of Scotland, *The Scottish Journal of Community Work and Development*, volume 3, Spring, 1998

Bryden, John, *Land Tenure and Rural Development in Scotland*, The Third John McEwen Memorial Lecture, Rural Forum, Perth, 1996

Burt, E. J., *Letters from a Gentleman in the North of Scotland*, London, 1759

Callandar, Robin, *How Scotland is Owned*, Edinburgh, 1998

Cameron, E. A., *Land for the People? The British Government and the Scottish Highlands, c.1880-1925*, East Lothian, 1996

Caird, J. B., & Moisley, H. A., Leadership and Innovation in the Crofting Communities of the Outer Hebrides, *Sociological Review*, ix, 1961

Coull, James, Melness - A crofting community on the North coast of Scotland, in *Scottish Studies*, vol 7, 1963, pp. 180-198

Cramb, Auslan, *Who Owns Scotland Now? The use and abuse of private land*, Edinburgh and London, 1996

Cregeen, Eric, The Tacksmen and their Successors, *Scottish Studies*, 13, 1969

Devine, T. M., *Clanship to Crofters' War - The social transformation of the Scottish Highlands*, Manchester and New York, 1994

Devine, T .M., and Finlay, R. J., (Eds), *Scotland in the 20th Century*, Edinburgh, 1996

Dewar, Donald, *Land Reform for the 21st Century*, The Fifth John McEwen Memorial Lecture, Rural Forum, Perth, 1998

Dodgshon, R., *Land and Society in Early Scotland*, Oxford, 1981

Dodgshon, Robert. A, *From Chiefs to Landlords*, Edinburgh, 1998

Douglas, T., (Earl of Selkirk), *Observations on the Present State of the Highlands of Scotland*, London, 1805

Dressler, Camille, *Eigg - The Story of an Island*, Edinburgh, 1998

Durckacz, V. E., *The Decline of the Celtic Languages*, Edinburgh, 1996

Edinburgh University, *Access to the Land - A case study Approach to Community Access to the Land Resource*, Centre for Human Ecology, University of Edinburgh, Ross and District Council and others, March, 1996

Flyn, Derek and Graham, Keith, *Crofters (Scotland) Act 1993*, Edinburgh, 1994

Goodare, Julian, The Statutes of Iona in Context, *The Scottish Historical Review*, volume LXXVII, 1: No 203, April, 1998

Grant, James Shaw, *The Part-Time Holding - An Island Experience,* lecture 1983, The Arkleton Trust, 1983

Grigor, Iain Fraser, *Mightier Than A Lord*, Stornoway, 1979

Hulbert, J., (Ed) *Land:Ownership and Use,* Andrew Fletcher Society, 1986

Hunter, James, *The Making of the Crofting Community*, Edinburgh, 1976

Hunter, James, The DAFS Crofting Estates:A Case for Community Control? in Hulbert, J., (Ed), *Land:Ownership and Use*, Andrew Fletcher Society, 1986

Hunter, James, *The Claim of Crofting*, Edinburgh, 1991

Hunter, James, *On the Other Side of Sorrow*, Edinburgh and London, 1995

Hunter, James, *Towards a Land Reform Agenda for a Scots Parliament,* The 2nd John McEwen Memorial Lecture, Rural Forum Scotland, Perth, 1995

Hunter, James, *Crofting Works - But it could and should work better*, Sabhal Mòr lecture, Skye, 1990

Jedrej, C., and Nuttall, M., *White Settlers - The Impact of Rural Repopulation in Scotland*, Luxembourg, 1996

Leneman, Leah, *Fit For Heroes?* Aberdeen, 1989

Lister-Kaye, John, *Ill Fares The Land*, Scottish Natural Heritage, 1994

Loch, James, *An Account of the Improvements on the Estates of the Marquess of Stafford*, London, 1820

MacCaig, Norman, *Collected Poems - A New Edition*, London, 1993

MacCuish, D. J., Crofting Legislation since 1886, *Scottish Geographical*

Magazine, vol 103, No2, 1987

MacCuish, Donald J., and Flyn, Derek, *Crofting Law*, Edinburgh, 1990

Macdonald, Sharon, *Reimagining Culture - Histories, Identities and The Gaelic Renaissance*, Oxford, 1997

Macdonald, Sharon, A People's Story - Heritage, identity and authenticity, in Rojek, C. and Urry, J., (Eds) *Touring Cultures - Transformations of Travel and Theory*, London, 1997

MacEwan, John, *Who Owns Scotland?*, Edinburgh, 1977

MacGregor, Bryan, *Land Tenure in Scotland*, The First John McEwen Memorial Lecture, Rural Forum, Perth, 1993

Macinnes, Allan I, The Crofters' Holdings Act of 1886: A Hundred Year Sentence? *Radical Scotland*, No 25, Feb/Mar, 1987

Macinnes, Allan I., Scottish Gaeldom: The First Phase of Clearance, in T. M. Devine and R. Mitchison, (Eds), *People and Society in Scotland*, 1, 1750-1850, Edinburgh, 1988

Macinnes, Allan I., The impact of the civil wars and interregnum: Political disruption and social change within Scottish Gaeldom, in Mitchison, R. and Roebuck P., (Eds), *Economy and Society in Scotland and Ireland*, 1500-1939, Edinburgh, 1988

Macinnes, Allan I., *Clanship, Commerce and the House of Stuart, 1603-1788*, East Lothian, 1996

MacKenzie, John, Land Tenure in Assynt and the formation of the Assynt Crofters' Trust, *Comunn Eachdraidh Asainte,* Stoer, 1997

Maclean, Malcolm and Connell, Christopher, (Eds), *As an Fhearann,* Stornoway, 1986

MacPhail, I. M. M., *The Crofters' War*, Stornoway, 1989

MacPhail, Isobel, One year on, the Assynt crofters are starting to see the bigger picture, *The Crofter*, December, 1993

MacPhail, Isobel, Sustaining Life and Land, in Mollison, Denis (ed), *Sharing the Land,* John Muir Trust, 1994

McCrone, David, *Land, Democracy and Culture in Scotland*, The Fourth John McEwen Memorial Lecture, Rural Forum, Perth, 1994

McGrath, John, *The Cheviot, the Stag and the Black, Black Oil*, Skye, 1975

McHattie, Angus, Crofting - Is There a Future? in Hulbert, J. (Ed), *Land:Ownership and Use,* Andrew Fletcher Society, 1986

McIntosh, Alastair, **Wightman**, Andy and **Morgan**, Daniel, Reclaiming the Scottish Highlands - Clearance, Conflict and Crofting, in *The Ecologist*, vol 24, No 2, 1994

McIntosh, Alastair, **Wightman**, Andy, and **Morgan**, Daniel, The Scottish Highlands in Colonial and Psychodynamic Perspective, *Interculture*, Summer, 1994, Issue 124

McNeill, Marjory, *Norman MacCaig - A Study of His Life and Work*, Edinburgh, 1996

Meek, Donald E, Gaelic Poets of the Land Agitation, *Transactions of the*

Gaelic Society of Inverness, vol 49, 1976

Meek, Donald E., The Land Question Answered from the Bible; The Land Issue and the Development of a Highland Theology of Liberation, *Scottish Geographical Magazine,* vol 103, No 2, 1987

Meek, Donald E., The Role of Song in the Highland Land Agitation, *Scottish Gaelic Studies,* vol 16, 1990

Meek, Donald E., *Tuath Is Tighearna - Tenants and Landlords,* Edinburgh, 1995

Nicolson, N., *Lord of the Isles; Lord Leverhulme in the Hebrides,* London, 1960

Orr, Willie, *Deer Forests Landlords and Crofters,* Edinburgh, 1982

Prebble, John, *The Highland Clearances,* London, 1969

Prebble, John, *Mutiny - Highland Regiments in Revolt 1743-1804,* London, 1977

Richards, Eric, The Sutherland Clearances, *Northern Scotland,* vol 2, Number 1, 1974-75

SCU/RSPB, *Crofting and the Environment: A New Approach,* Broadford and Edinburgh, 1992

Sheridan, Andrew, Native Woodland Management and expansion in the far North East, in Mollison, Denis, (Ed), *Sharing the Land,* John Muir Trust, 1994

Smout, Chris, *The Highlands and the Roots of Green Consciousness,* 1750-1990, Scottish Natural Heritage, 1990

Thompson, Frank, Land in Community Ownership - Sixty Years of the Stortnoway Trust, in Hulbert, J (Ed), *Land:Ownership and Use,* Andrew Fletcher Society, 1986

Thomson, Derick, *An Introduction to Gaelic Poetry,* Edinburgh, 1974 and 1990

Wightman, Andy, A perspective on landownership, *Am Bratach,* no 51 and no 52, 1996

Wightman, Andy, *Who Owns Scotland?* Edinburgh, 1996

Wightman, Andy, *Not For Profit Landowning Organisations in the Highlands and Islands of Scotland - Organisational Profiles,* Highlands and Islands Enterprise and others, December, 1996

Withers, Charles W. J., *Urban Highlanders - Highland-Lowland Migration and Urban Gaelic Culture, 1700-1900,* East Lothian, 1998

Withers, Charles, 'Give us land and plenty of it': the ideological basis to land and landscape in the Scottish Highlands, *Landscape History,* 12, 1990, pp. 46-54

Withers, Charles W. J., *Gaelic Scotland - The Transformation of a Culture Region,* London, 1988

INDEX